Chivalry:

A Study for Little Knights

Chivalry:

A Study for Little Knights

J. Aaron Gruben

Copyright © 2019 J. Aaron Gruben

All rights reserved. This book or any portion thereof may not be reproduced or used in any manner whatsoever without the express written permission of the publisher except for the use of brief quotations in a book review. Copies may be made of coloring pages, crosswords, and other activities for family use.

Scripture quotations are from the ESV® Bible (The Holy Bible, English Standard Version®), copyright ©2001 by Crossway, a publishing ministry of Good News Publishers. Used by permission. All rights reserved.

All pictures and photos found in the book are public domain. Every effort has been made to attribute correctly all the material reproduced in this book.

Printed in the United States of America
First Edition, 2019

ISBN 978-1-7339105-1-4

Cover illustration: Michael Howe, www.michaelhowearts.com

www.nmgrubens.com
www.posttenebrasluxbooks.com

y Chivalry Story and Activity Book

A book for _____ (Student's name)

Age and grade: _____

What I want to learn from this book:

_____

_____

"Sir Nigel Sustains England's Honor" by N.C. Wyeth, 1902

Table of Contents

Note to Parents	1
Lesson 1: Meet Guibert of Ghent!	3
Lesson 2: What is Chivalry?	13
Lesson 3: The First Commandment of Chivalry	20
Lesson 4: A Christian Knight	28
Lesson 5: The Second Commandment of Chivalry	33
Lesson 6: Two Churches	42
Lesson 7: The Third Commandment of Chivalry	48
Lesson 8: Protect and Serve	56
Lesson 9: The Fourth Commandment of Chivalry	63
Lesson 10: Your Country	73
Lesson 11: The Fifth Commandment of Chivalry	79
Lesson 12: Courage and Bravery	85
Lesson 13: The Sixth Commandment of Chivalry	90
Lesson 14: War Against God's Enemies	99
Lesson 15: The Seventh Commandment of Chivalry	104
Lesson 16: Faithfulness, Consistency, and Dependability	115
Lesson 17: The Eighth Commandment of Chivalry	122
Lesson 18: Honesty	128
Lesson 19: The Ninth Commandment of Chivalry	135
Lesson 20: Largesse	145
Lesson 21: The Tenth Commandment of Chivalry	152
Lesson 22: Your Quest	161
Epilogue	167
Appendix A: Answer Key	168
Appendix B: The Ten Commandments of Chivalry	174
Further Reading	175

Note to Parents

The goal of this book is the same goal I suspect underlies all of your efforts in educating your child: make them better people and better Christians. This is a character study. In it, you and your child encounter fascinating people and events from a distant age, both from history and medieval literature. This book may well open the doors to a lifelong interest in studying the past. But the main goal is not to teach about the knights so much as about the living code they followed. For chivalry is still very much alive today. And that's because chivalry is essentially a list of qualities that will help you become a better servant to God and your fellow man. It is codified Christian servanthood. While writing this study I prayed that it will help propel your child into the adventure of an active, thoughtful life of Christian service. Serving God and other people are, after all, the two greatest achievements our children can undertake (Matthew 22:37-40), as they are the practical outworking of their chief end in life: "to glorify God and to enjoy Him forever" (Westminster Shorter Catechism).[i]

But this is no ordinary character study. One of the thrilling things about Ancient Code Chivalry is that it connects us to the past in a real and exciting way. Though the details have been adapted for our modern age, you and your child will be learning to apply the same spirit of chivalry into your lives that a 12th century knight would have learned. If you choose to incorporate the Ten Commandments of Chivalry into your life, you will be sharing in the same eternal quest as the greatest paragons of knighthood in chivalric literature and history. You will be marching in step with great men!

Here are a few tips for using this book to teach your young child:

• Each aspect of chivalry in this book will be covered in two parts over two chapters, which are alternated: a fictional story about a page boy learning the concepts of chivalry, and then a more traditional lesson section explaining a concept of chivalry directly to your child.

• Take your time and have fun. I organized the study into 22 lessons. But there is nothing wrong with taking several days to go through one lesson or going several days without reading anything. You could split up the reading and activities into separate days as well. Take the time you need to keep your child's interest, and really make sure they are learning the content. This isn't meant to be a core curriculum, but a supplement to your homeschool: so make it fun for your kiddo. Don't feel bad about skipping activities either (like the "dust off your quill crayon" section if your child hates coloring).

- There is one memory verse every two chapters (covering one commandment of chivalry). I found YouTube song links to help with memorization for most of the Bible verses I've linked on my chivalry resources page.

- Always remember that chivalry is about action. Try to help your children put the commandments of chivalry into practice and build habits of living them. You'll find many of the study questions ("Think about it, talk about it" sections) and many of the "Quest of the Day" sections helpful for this. They've been designed to move the commandments of chivalry from paper into action in the reader's life.

- Try to help your child understand the difference between *historical chivalry* and *ideological chivalry*. This can be a tough concept for little guys, but it is vital to remember that we want to live the basic ideals of chivalry (the concepts behind the commands) and not necessarily emulate the same actions of knights in history. Not every knight acted chivalrously. And not every medieval application of a chivalric concept is appropriate for modern lives.

- Give your child a sketchbook you can set aside to use while you read the stories in each chapter if they enjoy drawing. I have included suggestions of pictures for students to draw as they listen to the readings in each chapter. Depending on the student, this may help keep their interest in the story as you read it and make things more fun.

- There are **periodic bold words** scattered through the daily readings. These are meant for your little knight to read aloud as you go.

- Most of the "Think about it" questions have answers in the back of the book in Appendix A. The questions with answers will be marked with an asterisk: *

- I have a page on my website with color versions for some of the pictures in the book and YouTube Bible verse memory song links. Go to: www.nmgrubens.com/chivalrykidresources, or just follow the link from the page for the study. The password is: littleknightservanthood

I believe chivalry speaks into our broken, modern age in incredibly relevant ways. My life has been made better as I've reformed and applied its ideologies. I'm thrilled to have you and your student join me and my family on the magnificent adventure of reviving the beautiful and ancient code of Chivalry!

J. Aaron Gruben

"What then is chivalry?
So strong a thing, and of such hardihood,
And so costly in the learning,
That a wicked man or low dare not undertake it..."
—from *The Life of William Marshall*[ii]

Lesson 1
Meet Guibert of Ghent!

Bible Reading
Hebrews 13:8
Psalm 78:3-4
Job 8:9-10

This strapping young **lad** is Guibert of Ghent. You say his name like this: "Gwee-burt of Guh-ent." And you probably say it's a funny name, too. But long ago, in Guibert's day, it was a perfectly ordinary name. He is 7 years old, and his father and mother have sent him to live with his Uncle Enguerrand (pronounced: "En-grr-ond") to start training as a knight. Uncle Enguerrand is a wealthy **knight** with lands near a city called Rouen, over 170 miles away from his home. In Guibert's day, it was common for families to send their young sons far from home to be taught by noble families how to be knights. First Guibert will be a page, serving in the household of his uncle while he learns basic skills. Around the time he turns 14, he will become a squire, and hopefully a knight when his squire school is done.

In this book you will read a story about Guibert, then read a lesson about the knight's code of chivalry. And the story starts today with young Guibert sitting in a bumpy ox-cart, rattling down a rocky road over a green and open countryside…

Guibert reached a hand into a slightly soggy tunic pocket and pulled out a small, **brown toad**. He was a lame toad, whom Guibert had rescued the summer before from a big feathery heron, and decided to keep as a pet. He named him **Zwane**. Zwane could be cranky, but it was nice to have someone to talk to.

"We are on the road, Zwane! Tonight, you and I start our path to knighthood!"

"Ribbit," answered Zwane. He blinked and rubbed his squishy eyes as if to say, "Faugh! T'will be no easy walk through a garden, boy! Believe me, I know about these things."

"Though, I doubt knights (or even page boys) are expected to carry toads about in their pockets. I'd best keep you hidden while I'm at the **castle**."

Guibert put Zwane back into his pocket. Roger the cart driver peeked back oddly at the boy, who seemed to be talking to himself.

The trip from Guibert's home of Ghent, to the **French** town of Rouen, took four whole days. But he was excited to see the sights and sounds of Rouen at last. Can you imagine an entire town surrounded by walls of thick stone and tall towers? Most cities in Guibert's day were like that. And most of the houses were made of wattle and daub, which looked a bit like stucco or adobe would look today. Rouen was an important seaport in northern France, and Guibert gaped at a forest of masts jutting up from the many ships which bobbed up and down in the **harbor**.

> Throughout the book you'll find scrolls like this with ideas for pictures you can draw while listening to the story…
>
> Draw Guibert of Ghent riding on an oxcart.

Guibert's father once told him the story of a monster called the gargoyle, who had a fat fish head and teeth and scales, and bubbled up from the sea at Rouen's harbor many years ago, and flooded the whole countryside by spitting out seawater. Guibert would have liked to explore Rouen's busy streets, but the sun was getting low, and he had to ride on to his uncle's fief outside the town.

Do you know what a fief is? A fief is the land a knight owned. It was given by the lord he served, in return for service (usually fighting in a **war**) he did for the lord. Enguerrand had a large fief, and in the center of it was a massive stone castle in which he and his family lived. Guibert passed through a little village full of rough hovels and poor farms, all were part of his uncle's big fief. His oxcart drove by a mill beside a pretty stream, and he tossed some of the bread his mother packed him to a beggar leaning against it.

A pascal lamb

At long last, he arrived! They were at the castle gates of Château Bon-heur before the sun set, plodding over the wooden **drawbridge**. Guibert stared at the long and colorful pennons (a type of long flag) that floated on the towers overhead. He liked the pascal lamb symbol that adorned the corner of the biggest pennon best. He felt just as nervous as I'm sure you would if you had to leave home and go live in your uncle's castle when you were only a kid. But he also felt excited. He was excited to meet new people and to learn new things. Most of all he was excited to learn about chivalry, the code of knighthood, and start his long training in the hopes of becoming a real knight!

As he got down from the cart, he heard the horn blowing for supper.[1] Roger bid the boy farewell at the gatehouse of the bailey[2] and turned the oxcart home. There was busy folk all around as Guibert made his way across the baileys to the **keep**— which is the house a knight and his family lived in. He passed grooms sweeping the stables, a laundress and her helper carrying baskets of laundry to wash, a smith pounding hot metal on an anvil before a roaring fire, a girl with a basket full of sweet-smelling herbs headed toward the kitchen, a boy herding foul-smelling **goats** toward their pens, and many more colorful sights.

When he came to the keep Guibert was ushered into the great hall to see his uncle. This was a huge, open

---

[1] Castle-folk in Guibert's day ate a simple breakfast early in the day: bread and wine (for the lord and his family and guests) or ale (for servants). Dinner was between 10am to noon, supper in late afternoon, and sometimes a "late supper" just before bed.
[2] A bailey was one of the courtyards of a castle, enclosed by the castle's walls. Many castles had more than one bailey, and Château Bon-heur had two, one inside of another (*inner bailey* inside of a bigger, *outer bailey*).

Lesson 1: Meet Guibert of Ghent!

room on the second floor of the keep, with a high ceiling and two fireplaces blazing in the far wall. The windows were high and barred. Candles and torches lit up the hall in a dancing, red, cheery light. There were painted tapestries and knights' shields hung all around. The floor was strewn with rushes. Three big wooden tables spread down the hall, each crowded with happy, feasting people. There was a separate table upon a raised floor at the far end of the great hall, where Guibert was presented to Uncle Enguerrand.

A castle's keep

Sir Enguerrand sat in a great oak chair with his family around him. He was a tall man and looked very noble. A **heavy sword** with a silver inlaid handle and cross-guard was strapped at his thick belt. Long dark hair fell out from beneath a circlet of silver and fell in waves down to his broad shoulders.

"Greetings, lad," he said. "Your father is a good man, and I expect you to learn well and do him honor. I'm sure you are excited to learn the ideals of knighthood and the code of **chivalry**, as well as the skills of fencing and hawking and many other knightly exercises."

Guibert was glad indeed at the sound of such exciting lessons and said so.

Uncle Enguerrand interrupted him. "But first you must report to the head cook for scullery work." (Scullery work means washing dishes and doing occasional kitchen jobs). "One of the boys has become sick and Cook is desperate for more help. It will only be for a few days. Then you'll help wait at table during dinner with the squires, and carry messages for my wife, Lady Ermingard." Guibert felt considerably less thrilled. Uncle Enguerrand saw the sad look that crossed his face. "Why so downcast, lad?"

"I was hoping to learn about knighthood, Uncle: not to wash **dishes**," Guibert answered.

> Draw a table with happy people feasting.

"Ah…" quoth Sir Enguerrand. (Quoth is a fun old word for "said.") He rose from his seat and stepped down from the dais, put a hand on the boy's shoulder, and walked with him around the hall. "Let me tell you a story, lad, that a priest told me when I was sent as a page boy to my own uncle's house long ago. 'Tis a story of our **Lord Jesus**. He had been betrayed already by that wicked man Judas and knew that He was going shortly to die on the cross. And it was then, before the very last supper Jesus ate with his friends, that He did something very knightly… Something that taught us the heart of chivalry. Do you know what that was?"

Boys in those days did not usually have the Bible around, and generally couldn't read anyway, so they only knew the stories in Scripture their mothers or priests told them (or that they saw in pictures on tapestries and stained glass). Guibert did his best to guess. "Did He practice swordplay with them? Did He teach them how to be valiant?"

Uncle laughed. "Nay, lad, nay! He did none of those things. He bent down, took the servant's **rags**, and washed the disciples' smelly **feet**."

Guibert was confused and said so.

"Right glad am I to find you honest and plainspoken, boy!" Sir Enguerrand commended him. "You see, Guibert, noble knighthood is for service. Before you can take up a sword and mount a **horse** in battle, you will have to learn well how to use your strength and skills to serve the people around you in more ordinary ways. The meaning of chivalry is 'armed strength in the service of the **unarmed truth**.' In the future years, I am going to teach you how to be strong: strong in many ways. But the thing you have to learn at the very start is to use your strength *for* God and *for* other people. Just like Jesus, who is God himself, and has all the strength and wisdom of God: and yet washed the feet of His disciples and served them. Now, you sit here and eat. Then get you to the kitchen, eh?"

After he had eaten, Guibert went with an almost happy heart to the kitchen. It was a short walk down a narrow spiral staircase, and out the door to a separate little building in the bailey near the hall.³ The minute he stepped into the place he was attacked by a barrage of strange smells: spices of all sorts, boiled meat on a hook, the smell of **hogs** roasting, the crisp smell of cut vegetables, and the strange scents of boiling broths and soups. There were fires all around the crowded room: three were lit inside little fireplaces set in the wall, over which iron kettles and pots hung on chains with simmering liquids inside and steam belching out, and there was one ruddy blaze of a fire in the center of the room over which pig carcasses turned. The head cook (who was named Buford) was a busy man, with hardly time to talk to Guibert in between his orders to the scullions—these were boys whose full-time jobs were to wash things in the **kitchen**. His wife (Dame Blanche) was with him, though she served the folk in the hall as the pantler,⁴ and came and went from the kitchen all day. She was a portly and worried lady, and seemed very superstitious⁵—but Guibert liked her.

> Draw a pig roasting on a spit over a fire and a big pile of dishes.

---

[3] In Guibert's time the kitchen wasn't in the keep—as it would be later in the Middle Ages. There was often a separate building called a "scullery" where the dishes were washed. A garden and fish-pond would be nearby. In the hall inside the keep were service rooms called a "buttery," where drinks were stored, and a "pantry," where food was stored for serving diners.
[4] This funny name does not mean that she sewed pants. It means she was in charge of the pantry.
[5] Superstition is a false or exaggerated belief in something otherworldly, like ghosts or black cats bringing you bad luck. Medieval folk tended toward superstition, often because they mixed up older paganism with Catholicism.

Lesson 1: Meet Guibert of Ghent!

Cook Buford put Guibert to turning the spit that roasted the pigs after he rinsed some dishes. It was hot work, and dull. Guibert kept having to swat away **embers** that shot toward him and singed his skin. But they couldn't burn away the excitement he still felt to learn about chivalry. This kitchen work would only be for a while, and it seemed almost exciting when he remembered to do it as an act of **service**. It was the first step in his adventure of chivalry!

In this book you _____ (write your name) will read about Guibert's adventures, and learn about **chivalry** along with him! Far from being a code only for Guibert's day, you'll find chivalry is something thrilling and useful for your life now!

Think about it, talk about it

Would you be scared to go live in a new house away from your parents like Guibert? Would you be excited to learn how to be a knight?
_____
_____
_____

What is your favorite thing about the Middle Ages and the time of knights?
_____
_____
_____

Why do you think knights would need a code to live by? *
_____
_____
_____

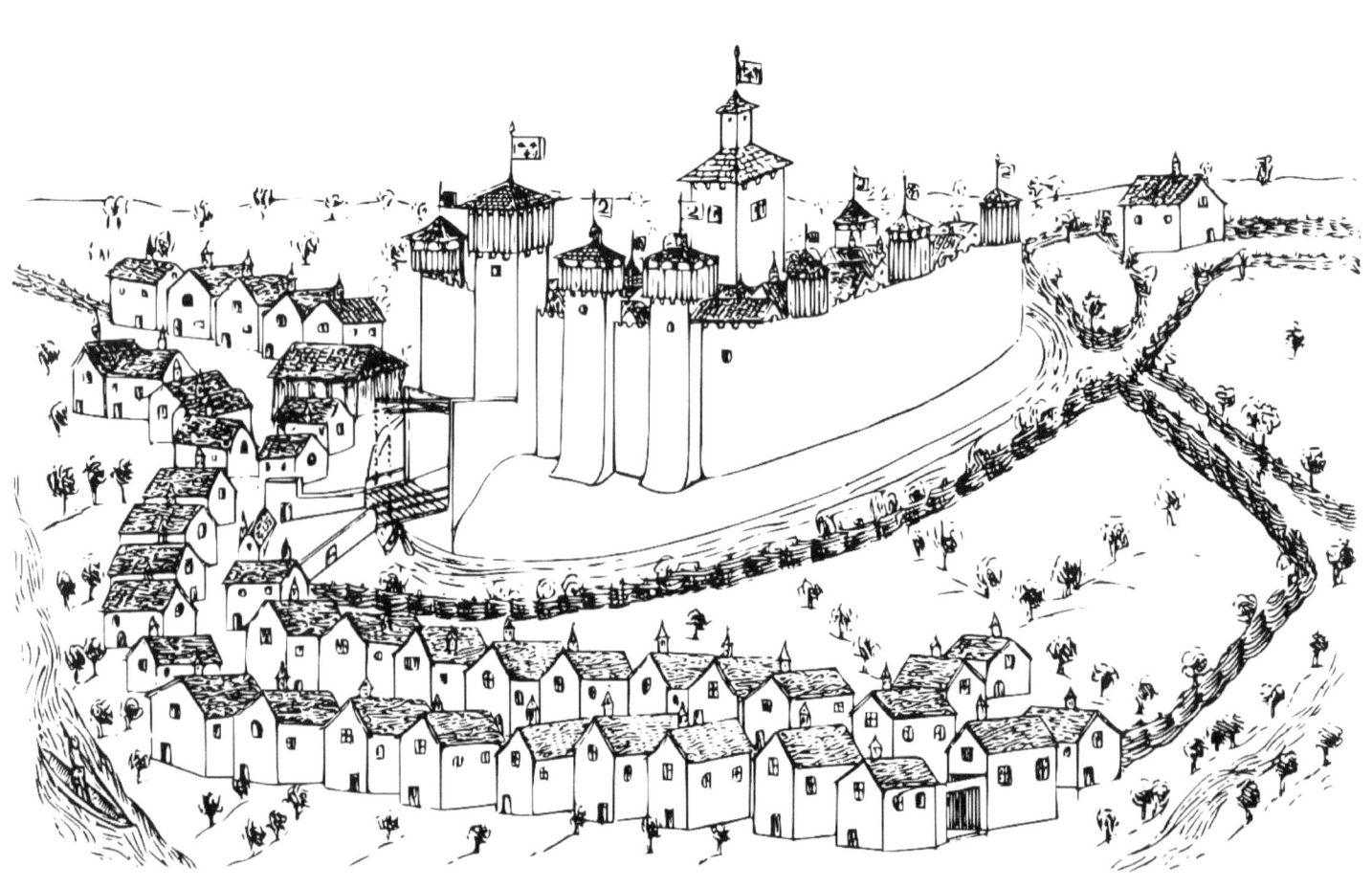

A medieval French city.

Lesson 1: Meet Guibert of Ghent!

Dust off your quill crayon

Color this grand-looking castle!

Quest of the Day

Rouen is a town in Normandy. Can you think of a famous Duke of Normandy who did something important in 1066? Here is a map of medieval France as it was during Guibert of Ghent's time. Draw a solid line from Ghent to Rouen to show Guibert's journey.

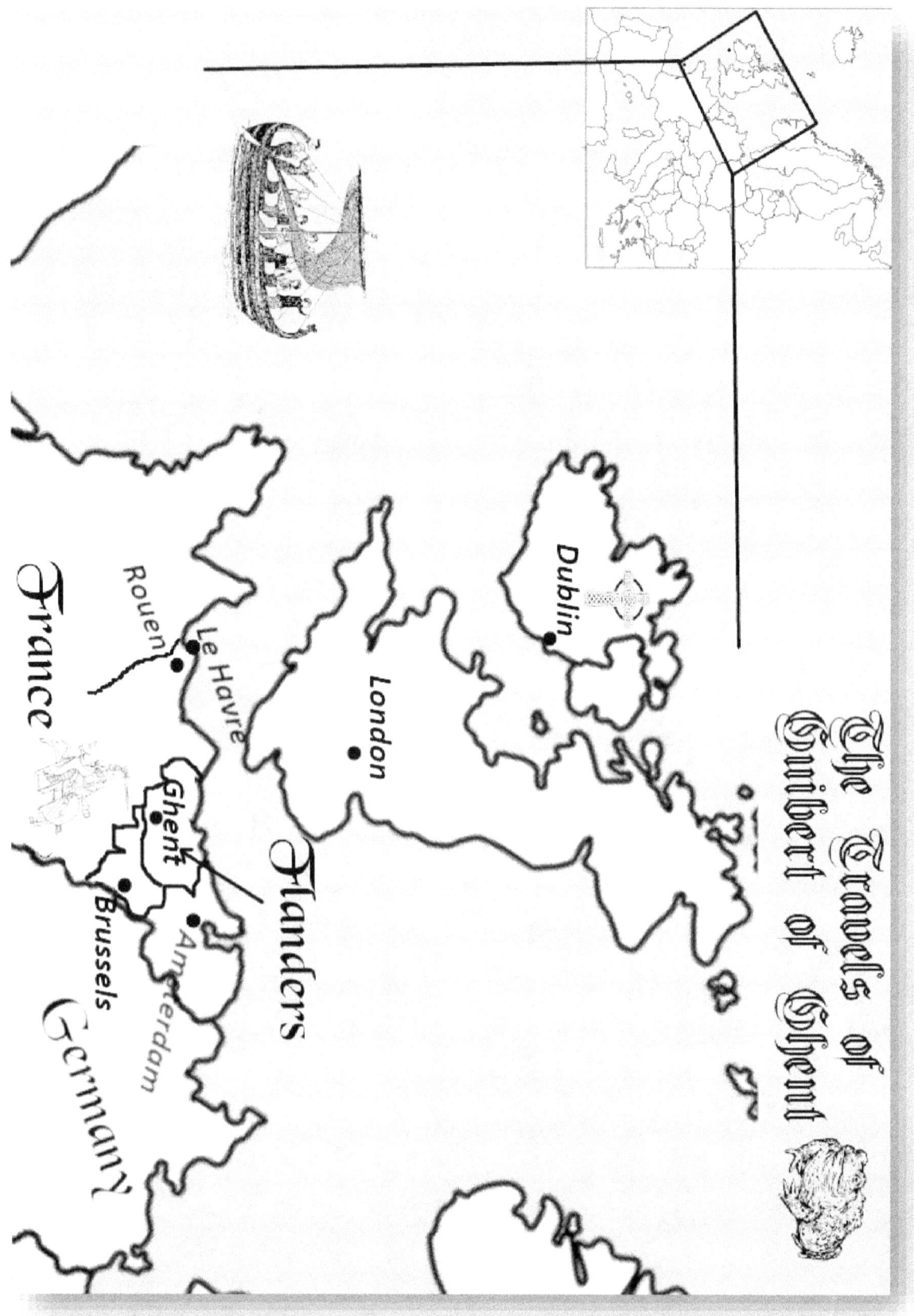

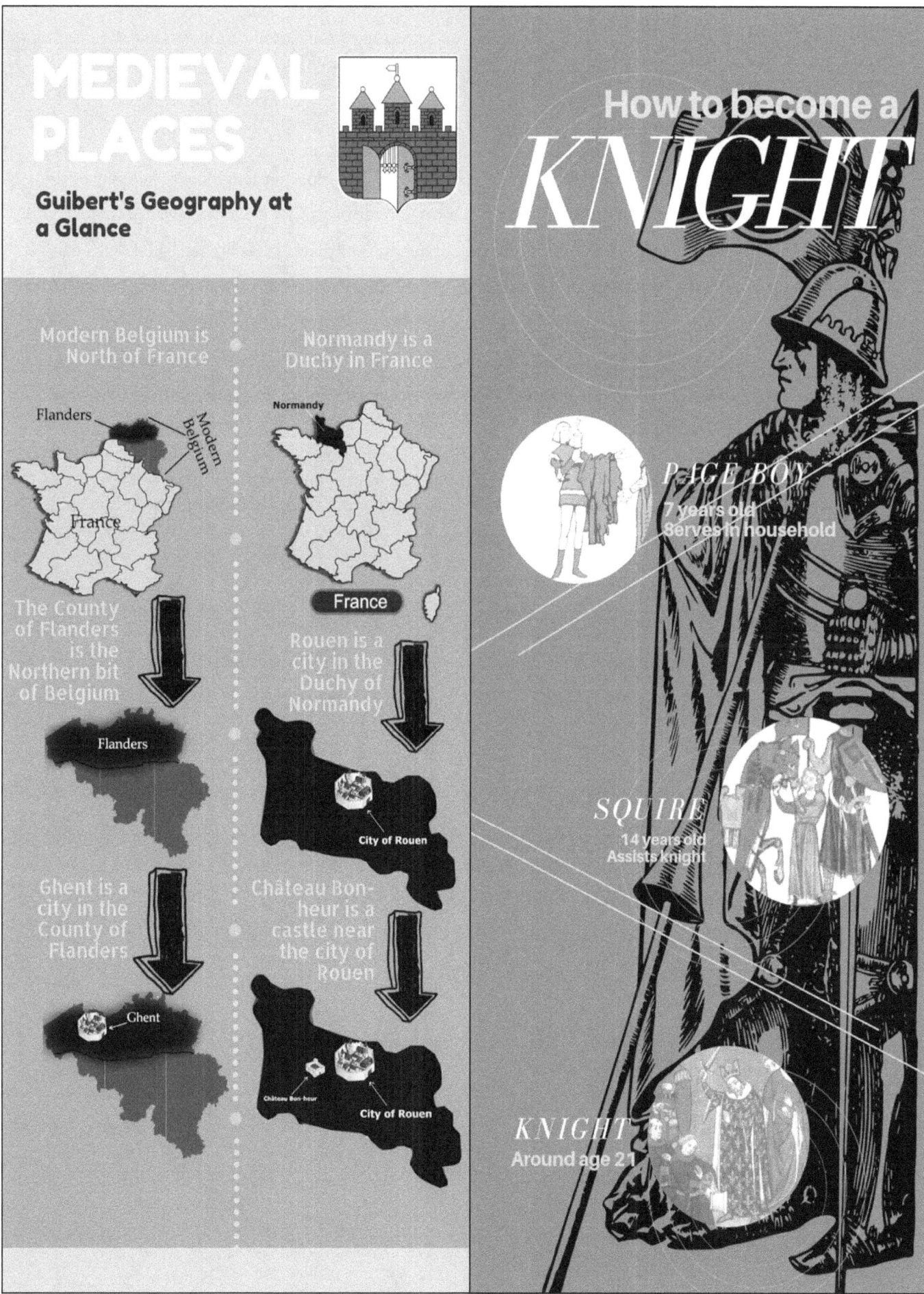

Memory Verse

"So then let us cast off the works of darkness and put on the armor of light." –Romans 13:12

Quotes

"I wonder what the boys of today would think of Myles's training. With him that training was not only of the mind but of the body as well, and for seven years it was almost unremitting… To make one's way in those days meant a thousand times more than it does now. It meant not only a heart to feel and a brain to think but a hand quick and strong to strike in battle and a body tough to endure the wounds and blows in return." –Howard Pyle[iii]

"A boy's life is very flexible. It takes but a little while for it to shape itself to any new surroundings into which it may be thrown." –Howard Pyle[iv]

"Society expected each man to aspire constantly to Chivalric Behavior; in return, they gave him an honorable place in the union of men." –Arno Borst, *Medieval Worlds*[v]

"What are words—empty words—in the balance with the deeds of the manly men?" –Frank Hudson, *The Song of the Manly Men*[vi]

Lesson 2

What is Chivalry?

Bible Reading

Judges 21:25

Matthew 22:37-39

Hebrews 6:10

What is a knight? Would you be a knight if you had **armor** or a **sword**? No. You might be a fighter with a sword. But to be a knight you would have to have special training, and be made a knight by another knight—and most importantly you would have to live by a set of rules (something we call a code). The set of rules a knight lived by in the Middle Ages was called chivalry. Even though it's been hundreds of years since knight times, chivalry is still a wonderful and very useful code for us today!

It's important, though, to understand that there are two types of chivalry. There is a *history type* of chivalry, which is the rules used by knights in their times. And there is an *ideal type* of **chivalry**, which is the reason behind the rules. There are no more fighting knights today, so the history type of chivalry is not something to live (though it is interesting to read about). But the ideals, the reasons behind the knight's rules, are still useful for us to live. The main purpose of this book is not to teach you about knights. It is to teach you about chivalry: the living **creed** and **code** of knighthood. And through chivalry, you can really share in the same mission and spirit as the best knights who lived and died years long ago. In the rest of this book, we will follow Guibert of Ghent's story as a page to learn chivalry with him. And out of the chivalry of his day, we'll discover the ideals of chivalry useful for us in our day.

The Middle Ages

What were the Middle Ages? Have you heard of **Rome**? The Romans had a huge and mighty empire that stretched over a large part of the world. They were the ones in power when Jesus was born. About 400 years after Jesus was born, the Roman Empire began to weaken and crumble away. Fierce tribes of barbarians with weird names like the Franks and the Vandals and the Goths tromped all over Roman lands. Eventually, Rome's empire crumbled away entirely. The Middle Ages are the years after Rome was gone and before the Renaissance and the Reformation, when more modern ideas and technology began to take hold of the world. It lasted about

1000 years, from the 400s (most people say 476 AD when the last emperor of Rome was kicked off his throne) to the 1400s.

It was in the wild and scary times of the early Middle Ages, just after Rome fell and the barbarian **tribes** were sacking cities and causing trouble, that chivalry started. Strong and powerful men in those days loved war. They hurt people and took whatever they wanted. There was no powerful government or emperor to tell them they couldn't do these bad things, and they didn't have rules to tell themselves they couldn't do them. But **God** had rules. God does not like it when people hurt or kill each other or take things from others just because they are too weak to defend themselves. And so, when the barbarian tribes became Christians through the work of God and the bravery of many Christian missionaries, they needed new rules to show them how to use their swords and strength in the right ways. They needed the code of chivalry, those rules for knights, to teach them how God wanted them to live nobly.

> Draw a picture of a barbarian warrior with a big ax.

Léon Gautier

The code of chivalry was not invented in one day. It grew over many years, and it was a long time before most of the knights agreed to it. It was told from knight to knight, and written in bits and pieces over many years, instead of being written down once on one list. This makes it confusing to **study** chivalry.

Fortunately, a man with a crazy long name and a weird job compiled the bits and pieces into one list to create the code of chivalry in 1883. His name was Émile Théodore Léon Gautier, and he was a **professor** of medieval handwriting. We

usually just call him Léon Gautier instead of saying his long name. You say his name like this: "Lay-own Gow-tee-air." In addition to knowing a lot about the handwriting of the Middle Ages, he was the smartest expert on a type of **epic** poems from France called *chansons de geste* (literally "songs of deeds"). These were story poems, telling all about the brave deeds of knights at the court of a king named Charlemagne. Léon Gautier went through these poems to learn what exactly chivalry was. He came up with ten specific commandments of chivalry, which is really great because now we can study and remember one list of knightly rules instead of having to read through all the books of the Middle Ages to figure out what chivalry was. We are going to learn how to live Léon Gautier's Ten Commandments of Chivalry (with some slight changes) in this book.

The Heart of Chivalry

A definition is an explanation of what a word means, and we should define chivalry before we learn more about it. What exactly *is* chivalry all about? Léon Gautier defined it just like Uncle Enguerrand did. He said chivalry is "armed strength in the service of unarmed truth." This is a definition of the **history** form of chivalry and was especially true for knights in the Middle Ages. Another way to say this is that chivalry is a way for a knight to serve God and other people using his strength and knightly training.

The simplest definition of chivalry for us today is this: chivalry is "codified **Christian servanthood**." This means chivalry is a list of things we can learn as followers of Jesus that will help us become great servants, or helpers, just like Him. Chivalry is a way to live as a helper.

You can see that, even though the history form of chivalry for knights was for boys, the ideas behind chivalry are just as much for girls as they are for boys. Chivalry is for everyone! It's for princes and princesses. It makes our lives more useful to God and our neighbor, and it makes life a grand adventure of doing good!

Think about it, talk about it

What is the difference between the history type of chivalry and the idea type of chivalry? *

_____
_____
_____

What are some ways the two definitions of chivalry (Gautier's and mine) are similar? *

_____
_____
_____

If chivalry is about using your strength, do you have to be strong to be chivalrous? Are there different ways to be strong? *

_____
_____
_____

What does it mean in the Bible reading that everyone "did what was right in their own eyes" (Judges 21:25)? Is it good to do what you want to without listening to anyone else? How was the time in Israel that this verse was written about like the time in Europe after the Roman Empire fell? *

_____
_____
_____

Lesson 2: What is Chivalry?

Dust off your quill crayon

Color this lovely picture!

Quest of the Day

Complete yon puzzling crossword! The answers are in Appendix A if you get stumped.

Across
2. Guibert's new city
4. The reasons behind a knight's rules
6. The rules a knight lives by

Down
1. The time of the knights
3. Scholar who wrote the Ten Commandments of Chivalry
5. A tool of a historical knight
7. The person responsible for making you chivalrous

Bonus Quest!

Build a Lego castle! Here is a real castle that looks a lot like Château Bon-heur. Can you build something like that? If you can, maybe you should grow up to become a Certified Fortifications and Siege works Professional Consultant! They are in short supply right now.

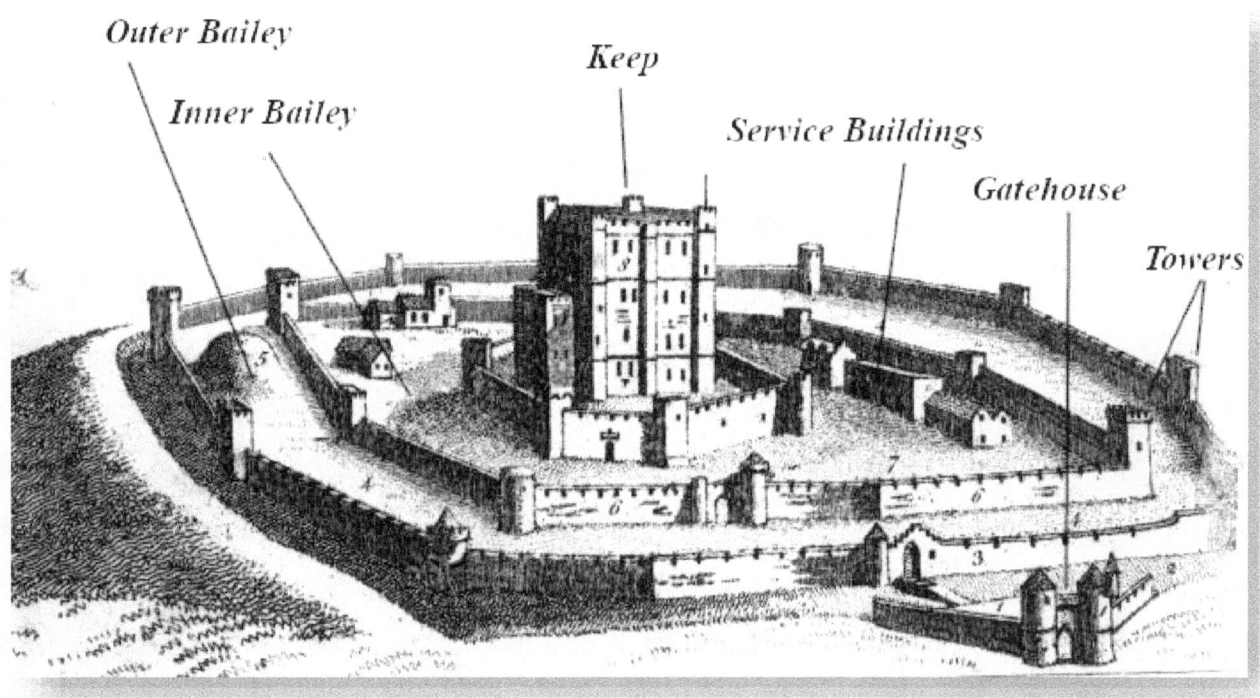

Quotes

"There is more than one kind of Chivalry, and lance thrusts are not everything! In default of the sword we have the pen: failing the pen, speech: and in default of speech, honor in our lives!" –Léon Gautier, in his preface to *Chivalry*

"Yesterday's the past, tomorrow's the future, but today is a gift. That's why it's called the present." –Bil Keane[vii]

"Chivalry is not just a fancy word with a neat meaning; it's a way of life." –Vaughn Ripley[viii]

Lesson 3

The First Commandment of Chivalry: You shall believe and obey the Bible, and shall devote yourself to Christ

Bible Reading
Acts 16:31
Romans 5:6-8

Guibert liked his first few days at Château Bon-heur, though he felt very **lonely** for his family and friends in Ghent. One day he met a boy named **Humbert the gatward**. Humbert was a clever boy, though he and his family were very poor, and lived in a tiny thatched hovel at a far corner of the castle bailey. Guibert met him when he was wandering the castle courtyards after his page duties were done for the day. They seemed to think alike, were about the same age, and quickly became friends. Humbert taught him the names of different types of plants and how to carve wood into figures and tools. The word "gatward" means **goat** keeper, and Humbert pretty much always smelled like the goats he took care of.

"'Tis a smelly job," Humbert told his new friend, "though 'tis but no messier than Ewerer's work!" Humbert laughed obnoxiously loud at this, evidently thinking himself very witty. But Guibert didn't understand the joke any more than you do. (An ewerer was the guy who carried water for castle guests to wash their hands or take a bath in. He was also in charge of washing the lord's clothes after hunting, so his job may have been messy after all.)

> Draw a big castle.

One day, after he finished **helping** Lady Ermingard clean the solar (a living room on the top of the castle keep), a priest in coarse brown robes found him. His name was **Father Thomas**, and he was in charge of teaching Guibert letters and reading. Guibert had hoped to start training for siege warfare or learn how to fight with an **ax** or something knightly and thrilling. But this was his school for the day. They worked on the letters from A to D, and Guibert was surprised to find shaping letters with his pen to be more exciting than he thought. He was glad, though, when Father Thomas finally said their first lesson was over. But instead of sending him back to Lady Ermingard, Father Thomas led the boy to the castle chapel, which was built into the castle walls over the gatehouse. Guibert's eyes widened in wonder at the

Lesson 3: The Third Commandment of Chivalry

> Draw an open bailey (courtyard) full of people and goats and cows in or next to your castle.

lovely colors. The chapel's floors and walls were covered in ceramic **tiles** depicting scenes from the Bible, dimly lit in the flickering candlelight. There was Moses with a serpent on a rod! And Joshua was marching around Jericho! Above a gilded altar at the front of the chapel was a wood-carved crucifix. The priest lit more candles and said something Guibert couldn't understand in **Latin**, while the boy sat quietly and wished he could play with his friend the gatward.

"Tell me, Guibert," Father Thomas said when his prayers had ended. "What is the first rule of a **knight**?"

"Um, er… Beat the bad men about the ears?" Guibert answered without much wit at all.

"Nay," the priest chuckled, "that is the tenth rule of a knight. The first rule, the First Commandment of Chivalry, is that he believes God's Word and devote himself to **Christ**.'"

"Oh," Guibert must have looked sad again because Father Thomas laughed aloud.

"Did you know Jesus is the Great Warrior who did battle against a **dragon** to save your soul?" the priest asked.

Now, this was exciting! Guibert wanted to hear more.

"First I will tell you of **Saint George**. I expect you've heard of him?"

"**Ribbit**," Zwane the toad commented from deep inside a moist pocket of Guibert's tunic.

"Er… What did you say?" The priest looked at the boy in surprise at the rude noise.

"I said…um….tidbit… I've only heard a tidbit… About Saint George, I mean. I've watched plays about him on many a Christmastide," Guibert stumbled over the words, as he quietly moved a worm from another pocket over to Zwane to hush his little toady mouth. It was very rude to bring a toad into a chapel.

"Well, George was a knight of England, famous for his strength and courage. He traveled far and near looking for injustice to fight, and people to help with his knightly prowess.[6] Once upon a time, when he came to a place called Silene in Africa, he found the people all sad. He asked them why. 'There is a terrible dragon plaguing our lands, poisoning our crops with his venom, and **munching** all our livestock for lunch!' They had offered the monster roast sheep every day to slake its terrible hunger and keep it from destroying the town. But the dragon only grew hungrier. Now it wanted to eat the king's daughter! George learned the

> Draw a scary dragon!

---

[6] Prowess is strength and skill in fighting.

poor **princess** was being taken to the dragon that very hour."

"I think that base and terrible!" Guibert cut in.

"Sir George thought so too," quoth Father Thomas, "and he spurred his horse to go out to meet her. He found her trembling before a huge, slobbering dragon with **slimy** green scales for skin and poisonous drool staining the ground. Its monstrous, bat wings made the wind a hot hurricane over the plains. So great was George's knightly **courage** that—where other men would have taken one look at that beast and run away—he set his lance in his arm, laced his shield, and spurred his hose forward to wage **battle**. It was a terrible fight, and George was wounded. But at last, he struck a death blow to the dragon, and it fell to the ground, making the earth tremble, and covering the dirt with steaming blood. The princess was saved, the king was grateful, and George was famous far and near for his noble deed."

It was a thrilling tale, to be sure, but Guibert was curious why the priest was telling it.

"The point is this. George is a picture of the **gospel**, young Guibert. After Adam and Eve sinned in the Garden of Eden, every man and woman and child after them became the rightful **prey** of the Devil: much like the princess who was offered to the dragon for lunch. Death and sadness came into the world. We are all born doomed to die and go into the burning realm of our master the Devil (who is shown in Scripture as a dragon sometimes). On top of that, we all **sin** against God every day and hurt His heart more and more. And we all must die someday and go to the horrible Devil after that."

"That's **scary**," said Guibert.

"Aye, 'tis. **But Jesus**, the Son of God Himself, came down from his throne in heaven and fought the dragon for us. Jesus is like Knight George. He fooled the Devil by taking your place and my place in death. Jesus gave his life on a cross for us, and He let God punish Him for our sins instead of punishing us. Then Jesus **rose** again from the dead and defeated our enemy the Devil forever. George fighting the dragon is only a story. But Jesus fighting the Devil is not. It really happened! We have only to believe this is true, ask him to live in our hearts and save us from our sins, and we are freed from the Devil's hands. Jesus will send his Holy Spirit to live in our hearts and give us **joy**. And then we need never

be afraid of dying, because when we do, instead of going to the Devil's lands where misery reigns, we will go to Heaven and be happy forever!"

"Wow!" was all Guibert could think to say. There was more to George's story and Jesus' story than he'd ever heard. Jesus' mission on earth made sense to him. He asked Jesus into his life that very day, to save him from his sins, and went away from the chapel **a new boy**. He told Father Thomas he'd have done it even if it had nothing to do with knighthood, but he was happy to hear the priest say becoming Jesus' friend was the first step of being a Christian knight.

"For now that you are a Christian, you will want to know God's ways and serve Him with all your strength!"

Guibert felt this to be **true**.

Think about it, talk about it

What does it mean to fight with Jesus against the Devil? What kind of fight is Jesus waging against the Devil? *

_____
_____
_____

What does it mean to say "chivalry is about doing?" *

_____
_____
_____

What kind of job would you want to have if you lived in a castle?

_____
_____
_____

Lesson 3: The Third Commandment of Chivalry

Dust off your quill crayon

Color this picture from 1515 AD of St. George fighting the dragon.

Another brave warrior in history was Alfred the Great. Here he is chivalrously fighting off Viking warriors to defend his people. Color the battle if your fingers aren't too tired.

Lesson 3: The Third Commandment of Chivalry

Quest of the Day

Find and circle the hidden words in this jumble of letters!

N	K	L	H	K	S	E	A	V	C	E	P	J	A	W	K	A
A	G	E	E	K	A	E	C	H	I	V	A	L	R	Y	Z	I
N	O	A	A	J	T	U	N	I	V	F	A	I	T	H	B	H
F	D	H	V	S	E	V	R	I	V	V	R	V	G	S	I	R
R	H	I	E	S	C	S	I	O	O	F	P	U	J	I	B	K
G	G	U	N	S	R	U	U	H	S	B	L	D	O	M	L	I
G	S	V	A	U	C	S	N	S	R	N	I	O	E	A	E	R

BIBLE   GOD
CHIVALRY   HEAVEN
FAITH   JESUS

Memory Verse

"For God so loved the world, that he gave his only Son, that whoever believes in him should not perish but have eternal life." –John 3:16

Quotes

"The Fairy Queen has sent you to do brave deeds in this world. That High City that you see is in another world. Before you climb the path to it and hang your shield on its wall, go down into the valley and fight the dragon that you were sent to fight." –Margaret Hodges, *Saint George and the Dragon*[ix]

"Saint George shalt called bee,
Saint George of merry England
The sign of victoree."
–Edmund Spenser[x]

"Jesus is not one of many ways to approach God, nor is He the best of several ways; He is the only way." –A.W. Tozer[xi]

Lesson 4

A Christian Knight

Bible Reading

Romans 3:23

2 Timothy 3:16-17

"You shall believe and obey the **Bible** and devote yourself wholly to Christ," says the First Commandment of Chivalry. Becoming a Christian is the first and most important part of being a Christian knight. If you don't learn anything else about chivalry in this book, I pray to God you'll learn this one thing: how to trust Jesus as your Savior and live for Him **gladly**. That's really what chivalry is all about! Jesus said the two important things in life are: 1) loving God with all your life, and 2) loving the people around you. If you serve God first, you can't help but **serve** other people well. The point of the rules of chivalry is to help you do those two things.

And the first step in the lifelong **adventure** of chivalry is becoming Jesus' friend. Have you ever asked Jesus to forgive you of your sins? (Sin is when you do bad things, or when you fail to do good things you should have done.) If you haven't, you can do it now! Talk to your mom and dad about it and **pray** a prayer to Jesus (who is God). Something like this:

"Jesus, I know I have sinned in many ways, and can never be good enough to go to Heaven by myself. But I believe that You died for my sins and rose again. Please come into my life and forgive me. Save me from the Devil and make me Your child. Thank you for loving me! From now on I will live as Your child, and follow your ways as best I can. Amen."

If you prayed that prayer (or have prayed it before), and really **mean it**, then you are a Christian. You are a child of God and a friend of Jesus. You are justified: a big word meaning that all your sins and badness are **forgiven** forever!

"Because, if you confess with your mouth that Jesus is Lord and believe in your heart that God raised him from the dead, you will be saved. For with the heart one believes and is justified, and with the mouth one confesses and is saved" (Romans 10:9-10).

In fact, when you become a Christian, Jesus becomes your **captain** in the knightly battle of life. Your main job in life, as Jesus' friend, is to march beside Him and fight what's left of the Devil's army. That fight against the Devil is the work of chivalry, and this book will help you learn some ways to fight better.

The **First** Commandment of Chivalry tells us we must devote ourselves to Christ. This means our most important goal in life should be to serve Him however we can.

"Whatever you do, **work** heartily, as for the Lord and not for men, knowing that from the Lord you will receive the inheritance as your reward. You are serving the Lord Christ" (Colossians 3:23-24).

Remember that chivalry is about **doing**! It is a way to live your life well in habitual acts of service to Jesus.

The Bible

But how do we know what pleases Jesus? By reading our Bible! He wrote down the ways He wants us to live our lives and we can learn them by **studying** and **following** His words in Scripture. This is the other part of the First Commandment of Chivalry. A chivalrous knight devotes him or herself to Jesus, by making it their business to study His word and live as it says. That's how we start becoming a true knight!

Think about it, talk about it

Do you remember the definition of chivalry? Why is it important to be Jesus' friend first, in order to learn chivalry? *

_____
_____
_____

What is God's Word? *

_____
_____
_____

Dust off your quill crayon

Jesus quoted his Father's words to Israel, to teach us that we should love God with all these parts of us (Luke 10:27, Deuteronomy 6:5):

- your heart
- your soul
- your mind
- your strength

Even though there's no liver or spleen on that list, it still includes almost all of you, doesn't it? And serving God like this is the #1, most important goal-behind-all-the-goals that we should keep in mind as we learn chivalry. The next page has a frame with Knight George killing the dragon to save the princess of Silene, which reminds us of Jesus saving us from the Devil. Can you draw a picture inside the frame that represents the four parts of a person from the list above? Then color the frame, cut the page out, and put it on your wall to remind yourself to devote yourself to Jesus with all these parts of you!

I'd love to see your drawing! (From this activity or other ones from the book.) If you want to, have your parents email it to me at aaron.gruben@gmail.com.

Quest of the Day

You don't have to be a grown-up to study and understand the Bible. Start reading it today! If you are going to serve Jesus through chivalry, you will need to know His orders. Reading the Bible can seem dull at first. But it isn't boring when you remember that the Bible is the words of Jesus Himself, the real true God, to you _____!

This is a quest you start today and try to keep doing all your life. If you don't have one, ask your mom and dad to get you a Bible. Start by reading through the Book of John in the New Testament. Can you read 5 verses every day this month?

Quotes

"Standing upon earth, thou art in heaven when thou lovest God." –St. Augustine[xii]

"The faith of these rude warriors, that faith which was so precise, had nothing namby-pamby in it: nothing dilettante or effeminate. We have not to do with the little sugar-plums of certain contemporary devotion—but with a good and frank wild-honey." –Leon Gautier, *Chivalry*

"*Qui en Dieu a fiancé il ne doit estre mas.*" – ("He who has faith in God shall not be confounded.") –Graindor de Douai, from *Jerusalem*, a *chanson de geste*

Lesson 5

The Second Commandment of Chivalry: You shall defend the church

Bible Reading

Ephesians 2:10

1 John 4:20

John 21:15-17

SWOOSH! THWIP! Guibert ducked beneath the sword **blade** that swung just over his head and stepped to the right to avoid a backstroke.[7] "Haha!" he cried. TWACK! WHACK! "Ouch!" he yelled in earnest. Guibert was quite glad the sword was made of wood and only for practicing with. It was the first morning he'd been taken to the lists, which is a fancy name for the field knights used to practice fighting in olden times. An old soldier named Pierre was teaching him the ways a swordsman should stand, and several of the many **longsword** guards he'd need to know. Guibert was only a page so he didn't get to practice long. But it was thrilling anyway, and he left with a grin to decorate his bruises.

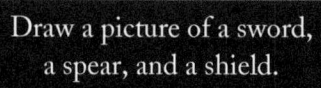

When he got back to the castle Dame Blanche, the cook's wife, fussed over his bruises and made him hold a compress of smelly **meat** to them.

"And next time you tell that Pierre not to hit you in the head with those wood swords, boy," she said as she bustled about the kitchen.

Guibert laughed. "But I have to get hit in the head sometimes if I'm going to really learn sword fighting, good lady."

"A young boy needs his wits around this castle, lad, an' ye don't want your mind dulled by fool things like bein' hit in the head too many times."

"Surely I'd be safe enough in my uncle's castle, Dame Blanche," the boy commented.

She dropped her voice to a whisper. "Don't ye say so, young Guibert! In this **creepy** ol' castle there are dangers you can't see with yer two eyes. Why, just last night I was woke up thrice by strange scratchings and gibberings inside the walls. Nobody believes me when I tells 'em, but…"

A longsword was a sword held in two hands, with a blade about 3 feet long.

---

[7] A backstroke is the swing of a sword up from when you swung it out or down the first time. You hope to hit the other guy with the backstroke before he has a chance to get up from the first swing.

Chivalry: A Study for Little Knights

"Ribbit," Zwane commented from Guibert's pocket just then, as if to say, "this one's batty as they come, Guibert! Believe you me, I know about these things!"

"Eek! Did ye bring a toad in my kitchen! Get it out, boy, get it out!"

Guibert scampered out quickly, chuckling to himself as he walked toward the Great Hall. Earlier in the day, Sir Enguerrand had told him to join the family at dinner, and it was nearly time.

It was a great honor to sit at table with the **lord** of the castle! At dinner, Uncle Enguerrand gave Guibert a good seat near himself, and they ate right heartily. When dinner had slowed, Enguerrand leaned over on one elbow, raised his bushy eyebrows, and asked Guibert an unexpected question.

"Did you know you have **Viking** blood in you, lad?"

"No, indeed!" Guibert had never heard this before.

"You do. You've a great great grand-sire named Asgeir, on my side of the family."

"Will you tell me about him?"

"Right gladly! He was a massive man stories say, all a-bulging with muscles and fair bristling with sharp-edged weapons from every pocket in his tunic. He stalked up from the Seine River to attack Rouen long ago. I'm sure you saw the Seine when you came through Rouen?" Guibert said he had.

"Men called Asgeir and his soldiers the **sea-wolves**. They roved down from the frozen lands of the north on their dragon-prowed ships and ransacked the monastery at Fontenelle in the days of your great-grandfathers.[8] The wicked Vikings loved to kill un-armed churchmen especially and steal the treasures dedicated to Jesus from the very altar of the churches. Asgeir and his men were so successful raiding and stealing that they hardly expected anyone to **resist** them… But a surprise awaited them one day." All in hearing distance leaned forward to listen, even though most had heard the story before.

"At the doors of the chapel at Fontenelle Monastery Asgeir met an uncommonly **brave knight**. He was a poor knight called Thiebaut—clad in hand-made leather armor (so folk say). He gripped in his right hand a battle-ax stolen from a dead Viking raider and a homemade shield of oakwood in his left hand. But though Thiebaut was not rich in gold, he was rich in chivalric courage. He stood **alone** to oppose the sea-wolves at the door of the church. He was silent and motionless like a tree, but he didn't have to say a single word. Just standing between the Norsemen and the church, standing like a wall of iron, spoke more words of **chivalry** than any

> Draw a Viking ship.

---

[8] In real history this happened in 851. Asgeir was a real Viking who took over Rouen and made it his base for raids through Normandy. Normandy became Normandy because it was given by a guy called Charles the Simple to a "Northman"—a Viking chief called Rollo. Don't laugh. It wasn't Rollo's fault his mom and dad named him that. Rollo brought his Viking buddies to his new digs, and by Guibert's day the country was full of folk with Viking grandpas.

Lesson 5: The Second Commandment of Chivalry

dry scholar's book could.

"A huge Viking warrior called Bjorn, full two heads higher than Theibaut, rushed upon him in a rage. Bjorn swung his ax, but Theibaut ducked below. The Viking ax stuck in the frame of the chapel door, sending chips of wood flying like a swarm of bees around them. Theibaut then wrought such a strong stroke to Bjorn's middle that he felled the man to his death in one blow! Seeing this, another warrior rushed forward and split a gash in Theibaut's oaken shield with his sword blade, while another thrust

an **iron spear** at him. SHOOP! THUNK! Theibaut barely dodged the deadly spear tip, spinning about. He hooked his ax around the edge of his foe's shield and jerked the shield away before felling another Viking in a single blow!

"Asgeir himself now rushed upon the knight, raising a massive, two-handed ax above his head with a mighty battle roar. His flowing yellow beard streamed out behind him with the rush of his charge, flapping in the salt-breeze like a banner of **death**. Theibaut turned as much as he could in the doorway and flung up his cracked shield. The oak split again with the force of Asgeir's blow, and the knight was struck heavily to the ground while his ax fell clattering away. But he leaped up again, and lunged at Asgeir, wrapping his strong arms about the Viking chief, bearing him to the dust in a struggling heap of wrestling arms and legs. Asgeir broke free with difficulty, but Theibaut hit him so hard with his fist that he was knocked down again. He snatched from the Viking chief a dagger that hung on his belt and raised it in the air. Asgeir thought he'd met his end.

"But then a Viking bowman let fly an **arrow** that struck Theibaut. Asgeir leaped up and killed the noble

knight." Guibert (and everyone listening) felt a pang of sadness to hear of the death of so brave a man. "But his death was not in vain!" Uncle Enguerrand continued. "Men say Theibaut's bravery impressed Asgeir so much that he spared the life of a nun and a monk and three children hidden within the chapel, and even left the gold cross at the altar, in honor of the brave man's deeds at arms…" He pointed a finger at Guibert suddenly. "And hear you this, page! Theibaut's **bravery** is a lesson to every knight that true chivalry is **defending** the church against her enemies wherever they are found."

"Wondrous!" Guibert said aloud. Who knew the past could be so interesting!

"And what became of the **treasure**, sir?" Alain, another of Sir Enguerrand's page boys asked.

"What treasure?"

"All the treasures you said Asgeir and his sea-wolves looted from the churches?"

"Ah! I suppose they took it with them back to the north or traded for things they needed. It's been long enough no man can say for sure. But that is not the point of the tale. The thing you must remember is that a noble heart, **stalwart** and knightly, and ready to defend the good, is worth more than any treasure! Can you remember that?"

Alain said he could. Guibert had scarcely expected Uncle Enguerrand to be such a good storyteller. The page boy decided he would become a brave **defender** of the **church** like Theibaut. And that night he went to his little straw bed with thoughts of brave deeds and feats of arms which rang all night in his dreams.

Lesson 5: The Second Commandment of Chivalry

Think about it, talk about it

Were the Vikings always the bad guys? Do you think they become Jesus' friends at some time? *

_____
_____
_____

Do you think you would have been brave enough to defend the church and the people inside from Asgeir?

_____
_____
_____

Can you think of other people in history who are known for defending the church? (Think theologically as well as physically.) *

_____
_____
_____

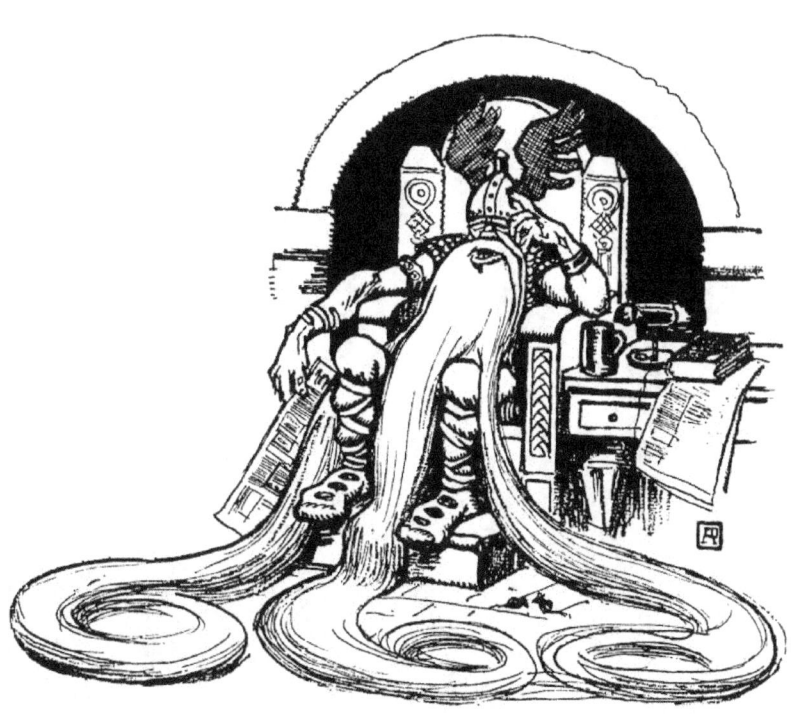

Lesson 5: The Second Commandment of Chivalry

Chivalry: A Study for Little Knights

Dust off your quill crayon

Here is a picture of a Viking King from

Iceland named Harald Fairhair. Color him and his fair hair!

Quest of the Day

Make yourself a cool Viking name tag! (Visit my website to download a color version!) Write your name in the scroll, cut out the picture, and wear it at the next Viking convention you go to.

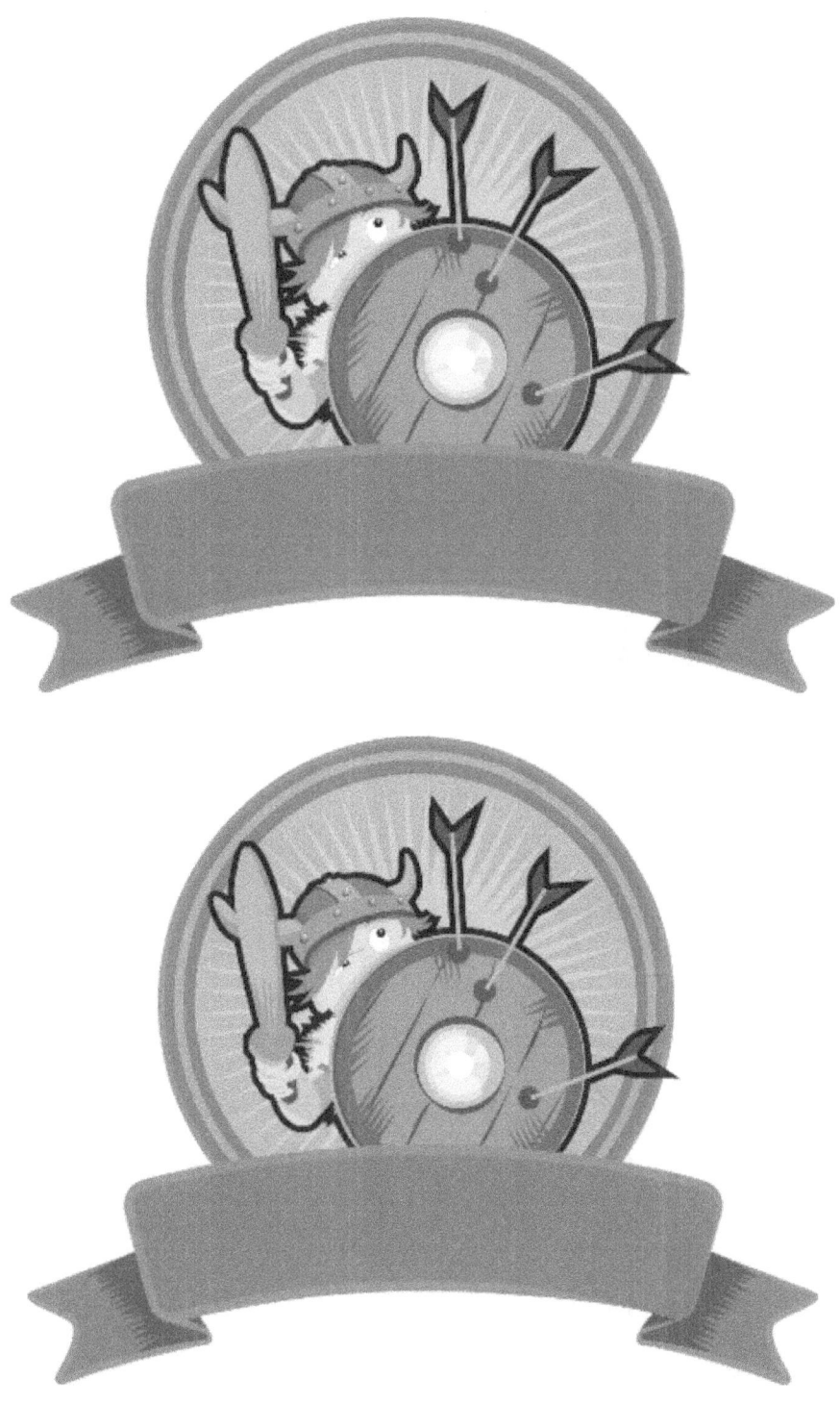

Bonus Quest!

Here are three types of helmets knights wore at different times of the Middle Ages—and a Viking one for fun. Can you make one to wear out of a cardboard box? For the epic, extra, knight-of-all-knights bonus, try to make all three!

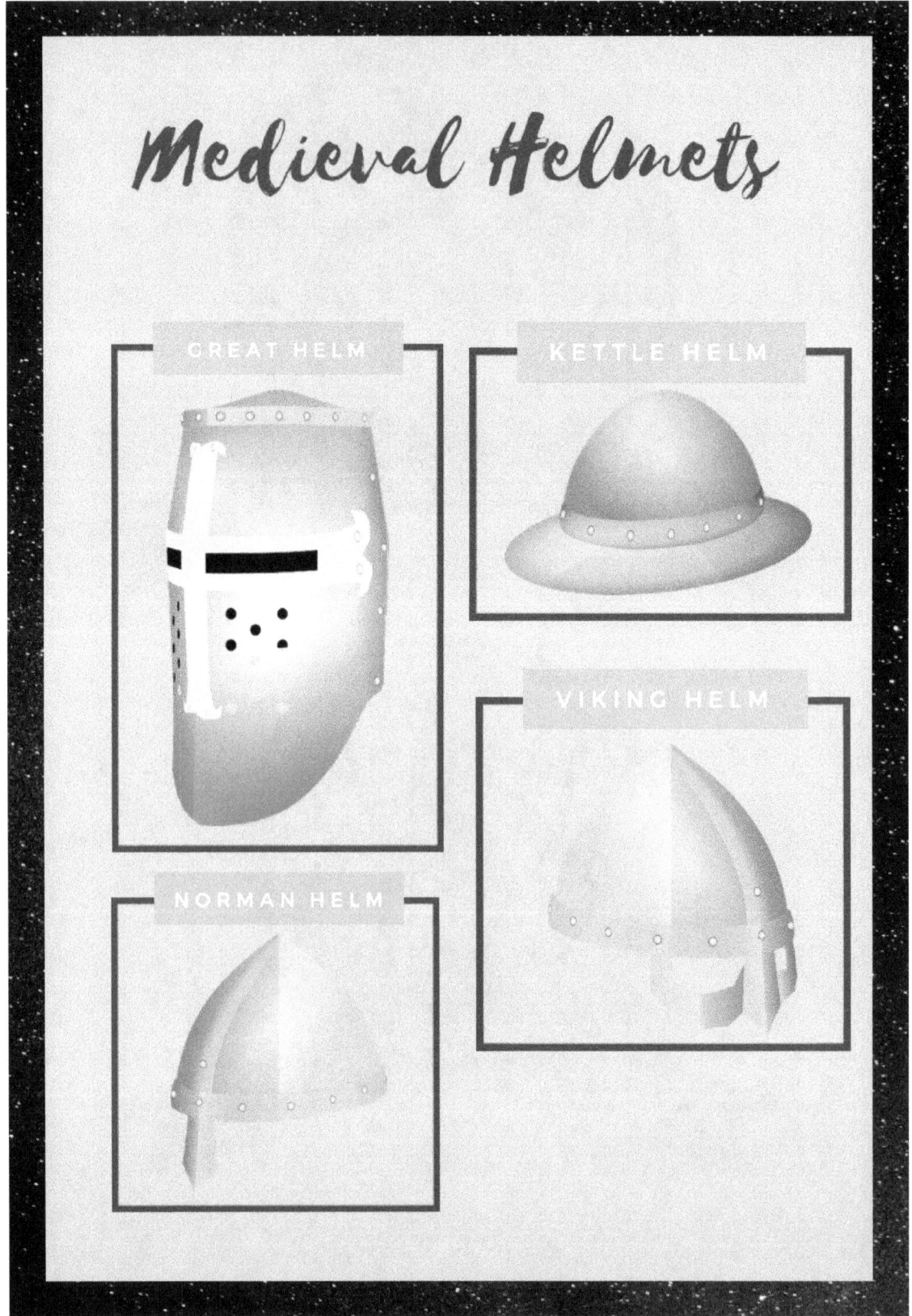

Lesson 5: The Second Commandment of Chivalry

Memory Verse

"Let brotherly love continue." –Hebrews 13:1

Quotes

"Happy are those who dare courageously to defend what they love." –Ovid[xiii]

"A dog barks when his master is attacked. I would be a coward if I saw that God's truth is attacked and yet would remain silent." –John Calvin[xiv]

From *The Boy's King Arthur* by N.C. Wyeth.

Lesson 6

Two Churches

Bible Reading

Galatians 6:10

Philemon 1:7

"You shall defend the **church**." What does this mean for you? You probably won't have to fight Vikings attacking your church with axes and spears… Hopefully not ever. But God still calls you, through the Second Commandment of Chivalry, to help defend the church He loves! Did you know there are two ways to use the word church? The big C word "Church" means all the people in the world (today and ever throughout history) who are Jesus' people. The little c word "church" means the local church, the congregation you go to in your **city**. Grown-ups sometimes call the big C Church "the universal Church." Your little c church is part of the big C, universal Church. The Bible pictures the Church (big C) as Jesus' bride. This means Jesus loves His people in every time of history and all around the world just as much as he loves Himself—and even better than your **daddy** loves your **mommy**. And if our Commander in Chivalry (Jesus) loves the Church that much, you should love it as well. You should care for your brothers and sisters in Christ, who are your fellow Christians. One of Jesus' disciples said it like this:

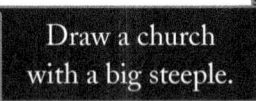

Draw a church with a big steeple.

"If anyone says, 'I love God,' and hates his brother, he is a liar; for he who does not love his brother whom he has seen cannot love God whom he has not seen" (1 John 4:20).

Being chivalrous means you will love the big C and the little c church: it means you should love friends of Jesus in your city, and even the friends of Jesus around the world you haven't met.

What Can I Do?

You might say, "I'm just a kid! What can I do?"

You can do a lot! Did you know that you are more than special? You are **skilled**. God made you with a specific set of skills and talents and abilities that he intends you to use for Him and to help his people. As you grow and learn about yourself, you'll learn more about these skills—and as you work hard in school and other projects you'll get new skills you can use for God and other people.

The main point behind the Second Commandment of Chivalry for today's knights is that we should use our abilities and skill to serve Jesus' church in any way we can. If you **remember** that, and keep your eyes open for chances to do it, you'll find there are many things you can do, even as a kid—in fact, there are some ways kids can help Christ's church better than grown-ups can.

Here are some examples:

- You can help keep kids younger than you **safe** at church, by telling grown-ups if they are doing something dangerous. Get **littler kids** *away from danger* first, if you see it, then speak *to their parents* next. This means you need to practice seeing danger. Get in a habit of paying attention to what's happening around you. (Do remember there's a difference between telling someone about danger and being a tattletale, which is trying to get other kids in trouble by telling on them.)
- You can encourage older people. A friendly smile from a young person, in particular, might really brighten up a grandma or grandpa's day!
- You can help clean up spills or put out snacks while people visit. Kids often have more energy and fewer distractions than adults on Sunday mornings.
- You can help younger kids be quiet during church services, or maybe even volunteer in nursery or to sit with a mom who needs help in service so everyone can hear **God's Word** better.
- You can talk to other kids, and encourage them to love God and obey their parents and keep the commands of chivalry.
- You can tell your mom or dad if another kid (or grown-up) shows you something bad, or tries to get you to do something bad. Sometimes grown-ups don't know about important problems that need fixed in a church.
- You can listen to the sermon and tell your pastor something you liked about it. Being a pastor can be a hard and discouraging job, and knowing the children in church are listening will help him press on! This goes for Sunday School teachers too. Tell them something you've learned and say thanks!

These are a few ideas. Use your imagination to find ways to help the church in particular. Look for things that need to be done. If you see something you can do to help, do it!

Other Brothers

Remember that God wants us to love His people all around the world, not just in our local church. You can learn about some of the problems **Christians** in other places face by talking to missionaries, or reading resources like Voice of the Martyrs, or getting familiar with other cultures and Christians through stories. Stay on top of what your fellow Christians are facing and pray for them.

Think about it, talk about it

What does the word "defend" mean? *

What if you don't like or get along with another Christian? Should you love God's people you don't like, or only the ones you do like?

What are some ways you see other people (adults or kids) help at church?

Lesson 6: Two Churches

Dust off your quill crayon

Decipher this dot-to-dot, then color the picture.

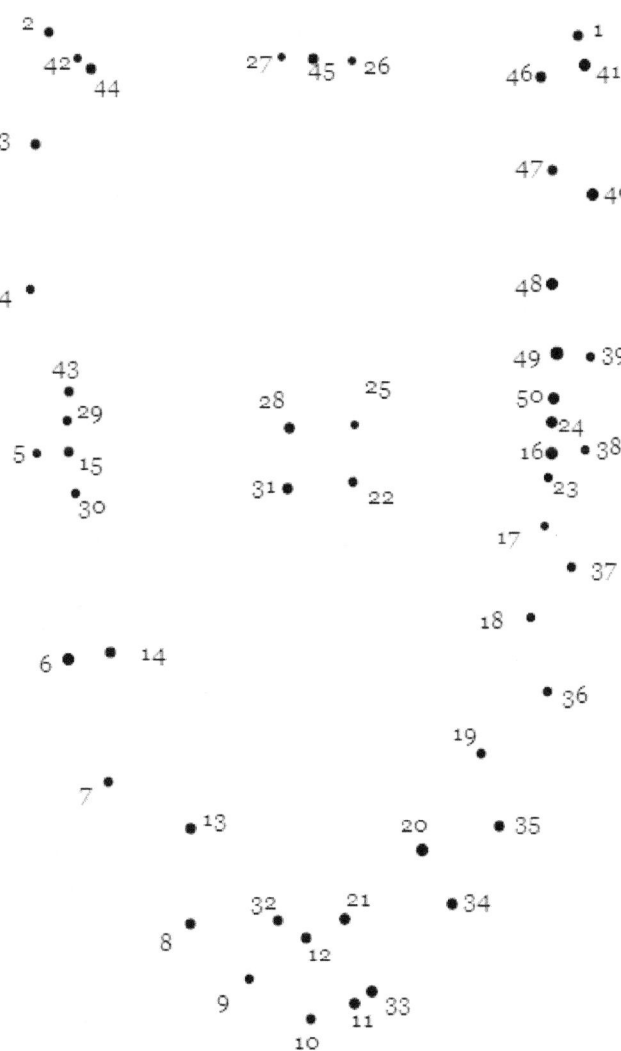

45

Quest of the Day

List 3 specific ways you will try to help your church this month. (There's a color version on my website.) Cut out this page, and keep it somewhere you can see it to remember.

Quotes

"Don't be afraid to defend the Church where necessary. Certainly the Church is not perfect… But in spite of its errors I would hate to see what the world would be like without it." –Martin Luther King, Jr.[xv]

"We must defend the faith. For what would have become of us if our fathers had not maintained it? If confessors, Reformers, martyrs and Covenanters had been indifferent to the name and faith of Jesus, where would have been the churches of today? Must we not play the man as they did?" –Charles Spurgeon, from his 1888 sermon, *Holding Fast the Faith*[xvi]

"Just as bank tellers need a thorough knowledge of legitimate currency in order to spot counterfeit bills, so Christians need a thorough knowledge of the Bible in order to spot bogus religious teachings. How grounded are you in the Scriptures? How deep are your theological roots? How capable are you of detecting false teachings?" –Charles Swindoll[xvii]

Lesson 7

The Third Commandment of Chivalry: You shall be gentle to those weaker than you, and become their selfless defender wherever you find them

Bible Reading

Philippians 2:4-5
Psalm 82:3-4
Titus 3:2

Guibert of Ghent did not like **bullies**. That's why what he saw in the little vegetable garden outside the kitchen one blustery morning made him feel so mad. A few little boys, 4 years old perhaps, were gathered around a smaller boy who was **crying** in the dirt at the feet of a bigger boy (much bigger than Guibert) who'd just pushed him down and taken a radish from the young fellow.

"Hey! Stop that!" yelled Guibert. He ran forward and **helped** the little boy up.

> Draw a big, fat radish.

Guibert recognized the older boy. It was Chrétien, one of Sir Enguerrand's two squires.[9] Chrétien was many summers older than Guibert, and he was not at all happy when the small page boy told him to give the radish back. "Go and make me, jack-o-napes, if you can!" he sneered. Bad boys called people ugly **names** even in those days.

Guibert paused only for an instant. Then he told himself nobody should bully, even if he was Sir Enguerrand's squire. He snatched the radish away and got punched in the eye for it. But the sound of the fighting, and cries of the children, brought some adults out of the castle. They quickly saw what had happened, and took Chrétien and Guibert to see Sir Enguerrand.

And that's how Guibert made his first enemy.

And that's also how the day's real **adventure** got its start.

Sir Enguerrand had the true story from his youngest child Odo, who had been playing with the group of boys and was angry at his friend's treatment. Much to everyone's surprise the knight was pleased to hear about how brave his nephew had been in defending the boy.

Later Sir Enguerrand had a private word with Guibert.

---

[9] A squire was a boy who served as a knight's personal assistant as he was being trained to be a knight. You usually became a squire after 7 years of being a page boy. And after being a squire for another number of years, you usually were knighted. Sir Enguerrand, because he was a rich knight with many relatives, had two squires and three pages at Château Bon-heur.

Lesson 7: The Third Commandment of Chivalry

"Well done, lad!" he said, as he patted Guibert on the head, in an **awkward**, grown-up sort of way. "You might make a fine knight yet! For one of the most important commands of chivalry every knight must follow is to be gentle to those weaker than him, and defend them without thought for himself. You've done well. I think you shall have the day off, and go a-hawking with my daughter Asceline." (You say her name like this: "As-eh-leen.")

And that's how young Guibert found himself riding on a bay palfrey, which is a type of girl **horse** people used when not at war. He had a really fun time, despite the sting in his left eye, which had become black and swollen. Asceline, a **cheerful** young lady about 14 years old, rode beside him. She held a splendid falcon, all bright browns and reds on his wings and chest, upon her wrist. A young man named Étienne (pronounced "Eh-tee-en") rode with them too and held a handsome hawk.

14th century mirror case from Paris, carved from ivory, showing a man and woman falcon hunting.

Have you heard of falconry? Have you seen a falcon before? **Falcons** are birds that hunt other birds and little animals. They're sort of like tiny eagles. In medieval times, people loved the sport of training falcons to hunt. Falcons were taken from the nest as babies and trained at a special place in the castle called the **mews**. Medieval folk would teach them to sit on their wrists with a little hood covering their eyes. When a bird flew by, they would take off the hood and send up the falcon to kill it. Hawks are a bit bigger than falcons and were sometimes used in falconry as well, and eagles were even occasionally used. We know a lot about medieval falconry today thanks to instruction books like *The Boke of St. Albans* from 1486.

> Draw a hawk, a lady, and a horse.

Guibert was delighted at the graceful flight of Asceline's falcon after she pulled its hood off and sent it into the air to catch a bird passing by. The falcon shot **upward**, wheeled around, and dove upon the partridge with a screech. A poof of feathers sprayed the air, and the two birds fell to the ground: right into the trees on the edge of a dark forest.

"Oh, faugh!" Asceline exclaimed. "Now I shall have to ride over and find little Petrus." (For this was the name of her falcon).

"Faugh!" Zwane echoed. But it sounded more like "**Ribbit!**" to the children.

Just then a fat **rabbit** scampered by, and Étienne glanced longingly at it. Asceline laughed and said she would be fine retrieving Petrus. He nodded quickly before releasing his hawk.

"I can go with you," offered Guibert. He and Asceline rode across the lush meadow into the forest together. The trees were very thick, but they found a little path near where they'd seen the falcon last. A faint jingling sound (from the little bells attached to Petrus' feet) led them through the maze of tree trunks and beneath the dark canopy of the forest. The **jingling** grew louder and louder. They dismounted and led their horses so as not to frighten the bird. But when the woods opened to a little clearing in the trees they met a surprising sight.

Two big, rather rough-looking fellows, clothed in tattered cloaks and woolen jerkins, stood arguing with each other. One held a dead partridge. One held Petrus the falcon on his hand and was feeding him a bit of meat. Both stopped arguing and smiled wickedly as the children entered the wooded clearing.

"Excuse me, sirrahs! That's my **falcon**," Asceline called to them.

"Oh, 'tis it?" one of them (whose greasy black hair fell over his right eye) spoke with a gravelly voice.

"We done found it, 'tis our falcon now," inserted the other fellow (who had no hair at all to fall over his eye) in a high-pitched, mousy tone. "And a nice price it'll fetch us at Lord Talcott's court."

"Lord Talcott, indeed!" Asceline exclaimed in disgust. She dropped the reins and walked toward them boldly. Guibert felt nervous. "Even such an enemy of my father as he would hardly buy stolen goods from the likes of you."

Guibert dropped his horse's reins too, and moved forward angrily. "You cannot rob a lady! That would be most **unmanly** of you." Both men pulled long knives from their belts, and Guibert's nervous feeling turned into icy fear in his heart. He wondered if a lady's falcon was worth dying over. He briefly thought of running away without Asceline or her bird, though he knew he should stay. Then something terrible and unexpected happened before he could decide.

The **thumpitty-clop** sound of horse hooves sounded through the soft forest floor, and a familiar voice rang out behind them. "As you yourself will be coming to Lord Talcott's court, fair Asceline, I'm certain he would not mind buying Petrus for you." It was Étienne, and Guibert did not like the look on his face at all. Asceline demanded to know what he meant. "Sir Talcott means for you **marry** him." Asceline's face went white. "Sir Talcott is my liege-lord,[10] and sent me to your father's castle to find a way to bring you to him."

Guibert moved closer to Asceline, who was backing away from the men now with horror on her face. She was moving toward their horses but the two children had already stepped far away from their steeds. He

---

[10] A liege-lord was a medieval guy's boss. A "vassal" was a less powerful man who promised his service for money or land.

wondered how the two of them would escape.

"I hired these two ruffians to bait your falcon and **lure** you far from the castle."

Étienne pulled out a sword from his belt and started to ride toward them. Guibert reached unnoticed into a pouch hanging from Asceline's belt and brought out a bit of the raw meat she had as bait for her falcon.

"This lad wasn't meant to be here, but that's easily remedied. He'll soon be past talking."

Another **frozen** chill went through Guibert's heart at those sinister words, and he thought again of running away as far as he could right then. His chances of getting away from this trap alive would be better if he left Asceline behind. But his chivalrous (and quaking) spirit hated that idea. He knew he could not leave a lady undefended.

And so…

Guibert made his move.

Quick and unexpected as the strike of snake, Guibert threw the meat in his hand right into Étienne's face. This was surprising enough. But the meat was (as Guibert had hoped) followed immediately by a flutter of wings and talons. Petrus the falcon let out a screech and flung himself away from the brigand's arm to snatch the bait. Étienne screamed aloud and clawed at the bird.

Chaos ensued.

Étienne's horse panicked at the screaming flapping bird and the screaming man in the saddle. It reared with a whinny, threw Étienne down, and dashed away into the woods. The children's horses panicked too and followed Étienne's horse toward the castle.

But the chaos was what Guibert and Asceline needed. Guibert grabbed Asceline's hand, shouted, "Follow me!" and both he and the girl dashed into the woods as fast as they could run.

Unfortunately, the direction leading away from the traitorous Étienne and his thugs also led away from Uncle Enguerrand's castle. They were running straight into the heart of the deep, dark woodlands…

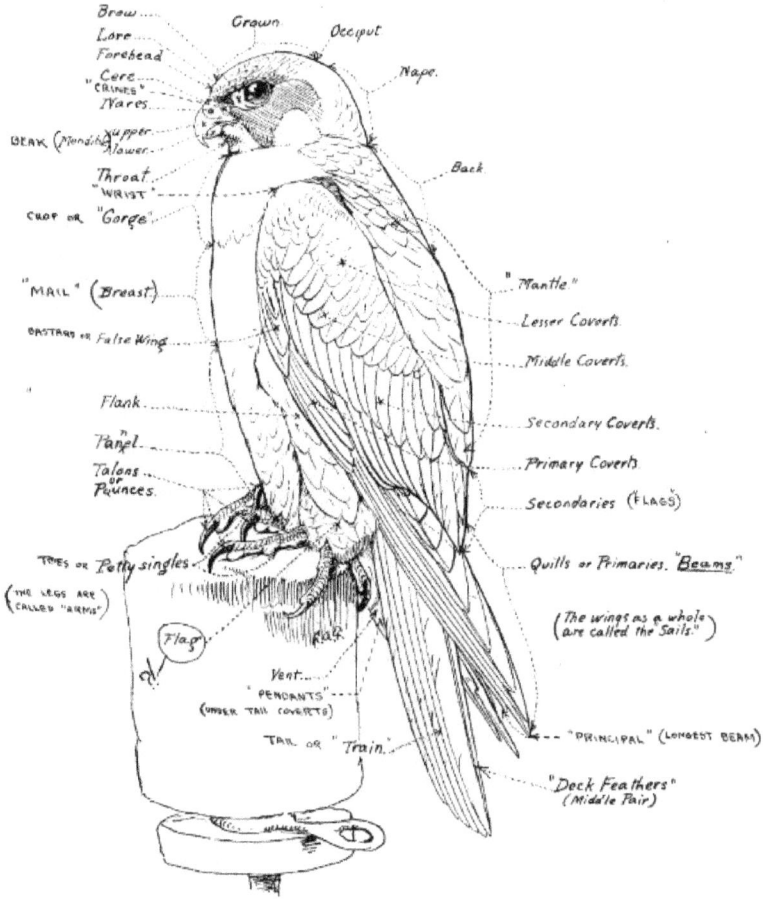

Think about it, talk about it

Why do many people in Guibert's story have funny-sounding names? Can you think of other medieval names?*
_____
_____
_____

How did Guibert live the Third Commandment of Chivalry in this chapter? *
_____
_____
_____

Who are people in your life you can protect?
_____
_____
_____

Lesson 7: The Third Commandment of Chivalry

Dust off your quill crayon

Quest of the Day

Get this knight safely to his castle by completing the maze!

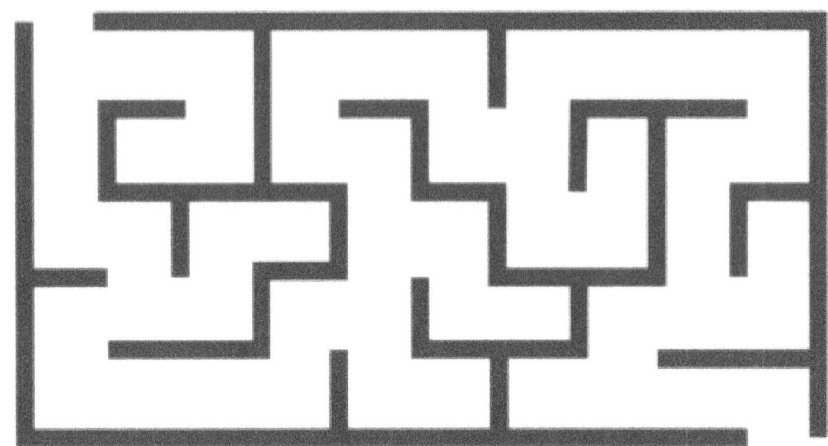

Memory Verse

"Do nothing from selfish ambition or conceit, but in humility count others more significant than yourselves." –Philippians 2:3

Quotes

"If you find a man, or a woman, or an orphan or a lady, in any kind of distress, you'll do well to lend them your aid if you know how and are able." –Sir Percival's mother (Chrétin de Troyes as quoted by Frances Gies)[xviii]

"Defend the weak, protect both young and old, never desert your friends. Give justice to all, be fearless in battle and always ready to defend the right." –Law of the Badger Lords (Brian Jacques)[xix]

"It is excellent to have a giant's strength but it is tyrannous to use it like a giant." –William Shakespeare, *Measure for Measure*[xx]

Lesson 7: The Third Commandment of Chivalry

"But no generous mind delights to oppress the weak, but rather to cherish and protect." –Anne Bronte[xxi]

"To risk life to save a smile on a face of a woman or a child is the secret of chivalry." –Dejan Stojanovic[xxii]

Lesson 8

Protect and Serve

Bible Reading

Proverbs 31:8-9

Hebrews 4:15

The Third Commandment of Chivalry says, "You shall be **gentle** to those weaker than you, and become their selfless defender wherever you find them." It teaches us to **protect** those weaker and to be their **defender**. This is a commandment for boys and girls everywhere. Sometimes this will mean standing up dramatically and defending others against some kind of harm. Guibert did this when he stayed and fought Étienne for Asceline. But it will more often mean doing little things to protect those weaker from the troubles that come from their weakness. It also teaches us to serve the weak with our strength. Strength can mean physical strength, but it also means strength in our minds or our skills and talents.

In Luke 2:52 we are told that a young Jesus "increased in wisdom and in stature and in favor with God and man." This is the only place we read in Scripture about Jesus between his birth and the beginning of His ministry at 30. As a young man, we know that **Jesus grew** mentally, physically, and socially. He is a good model to follow, and indeed we must follow His model if we are going to practice chivalry to the greatest extent we can. **Grow** your mind and learn to be wise. Grow in stature, which means you need to take care of your body. Grow with God by reading the Bible and praying. Grow in favor with others by being social, even if it's hard to do—don't just sit in your house on the phone or watching TV most of the time.

Gentleness

The Third Commandment of Chivalry teaches us to be gentle. Gentleness is not being weak or **fluffy**. Gentleness is the power to control your strength and to use it to protect and not harm those weaker than you.

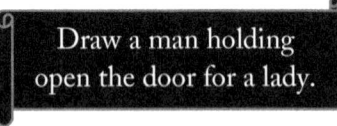

Who is weaker than you? Your little brother or sister is weaker than you are. You should never hurt babies or little children. Guibert showed this quality when he protected the little boy. Instead of hurting little kids, you should help protect them and keep them safe. Girls are usually weaker than boys. The Bible teaches us to respect and protect girls. If you are a boy, you must never hurt or hit a girl. Instead, you should help **protect** her and keep her safe. Guibert did this when he offered to ride with Asceline so she wouldn't be alone looking for her bird in the woods. Are you extra smart, maybe smarter than other people? Your brain is strong in that case, and you can use your strong brain to help people with weaker brains learn better! Do you have a friend with a disability, an illness that makes it hard for them to do something you can do? Then you can help them by doing that thing for them! Remember chivalry is about serving others like Jesus does. The Third Commandment is about using our strength to serve others where they are weaker.

Selflessness

The Third Commandment of Chivalry teaches us to be **selfless**. Selflessness is the power to do things for other people before we do things for ourselves. It is the opposite of selfishness, which is caring more often about what you want than what other people want. God does not want you to be a selfish person. He wants you to care about others more than you care about yourself. This is the main thing you need to do: put other people ahead of yourself. Jesus is the best example of selflessness! He left his **glory** and riches in Heaven to be born in a cold, stinky stable, and then grew up and died on a cross for you and me. He put the forgiveness and salvation you and I needed before His own safety or comfort.

There are many ways we can live lives of gentleness and selflessness. Some are big things, and some are very little things we can do—things people may not even notice. But that's ok! We are trying to help people and be servants like Jesus, not get noticed. And we know that **God notices** our good works of service even when other people don't. Be always looking around you, trying to notice when someone (especially someone weaker) needs help. (Don't be a self-absorbed person like this strange-looking knight!) Use your creativity and your imagination to think of ways to help. Here are some things you could do:

- Clean the house for your mom when she's tired.
- Help your little brother carry a heavy toy.
- Stand up and offer a lady your seat or open the door for her.
- Be polite to everyone.
- Get yourself ready to defend someone in need, by doing things like exercising to keep your body fit, or learning self-defense skills.
- Decide not to hit your little brother or sister (or anyone). Boys: do not hit a girl ever.
- Help push a friend's wheelchair.
- Help teach a friend something they are having trouble learning in school.
- Stand up to bullying for someone weaker.
- Pull your baby sibling away from wall sockets or other dangerous things (and tell your mom).

There are dozens of ways to protect and serve people weaker than ourselves. We have to **decide** ahead of time we will be chivalrous people ready to protect and serve where we can: and then be on the lookout for those chances. You can see that a big part of this commandment is deciding how we will treat those weaker than us. We must make the decision to never bully anyone or hit girls or younger people, or anyone weaker than us.

Courtesy

One way we serve others is by courtesy. Many of the rules of **polite** behavior we think of today come from the Third Commandment of Chivalry as ways to show everyone we are ready to serve and protect those who are weaker. Being polite is, at its core, a way of treating others with gentleness and selflessness. It is a way to honor other people.

Strength

We are called to be strong for others. To be chivalrous you must learn strength. You need to learn the *strength of body*. Exercise regularly and try to be in shape. Work to develop endurance. Endurance is toughness. It is the ability to keep on through **hard** or painful things without complaining. You need to learn the *strength of heart*. A true knight of chivalry is tough and does not whine. He is strong of heart. And because of this, he is someone that his friends can lean on in their troubles.

Think about it, talk about it

What are habits? How is a habit important in learning the Third Commandment of Chivalry? *

_____
_____
_____

Do you know any rules of polite behavior? Talk to your parents about this, and try to get in the habit of doing them.

_____
_____
_____

Who are some people in your life who are weaker (maybe just think about them and don't write them down on the page: we also don't want to ever make someone feel sad by telling them we think they are weak). What are some ways you can protect and help them? (This you can write down to help you remember your action plan.)

_____
_____
_____

Dust off your quill crayon

Quest of the Day

Make a plan! Write down some ways you will start defending those weaker, or how you will prepare yourself to defend them. Will you help your brother learn to clean his room? Will you take a class in self-defense or martial arts with your dad? Write on the picture below 3 (or more) things you will start trying to make into habits (something you do over and over again until you can do it without thinking about it).

Quotes

"Some say that the age of chivalry is past, that the spirit of romance is dead. The age of chivalry is never past, so long as there is a wrong left unredressed on earth." –Charles Kingsley[xxiii]

"…To help other people at all times;
To keep myself physically strong,
Mentally awake, and morally straight."
–from the Boy Scout Oath[xxiv]

"Strength, if not used to protect, is but weakness." –Lewis F. Korns, *Thoughts*[xxv]

"You have power over your mind—not outside events. Realize this, and you will find strength." –Marcus Aurelius, *Meditations*[xxvi]

"As the stones in an arch help to strengthen one another, one Christian by imparting his experience, heats and quickens another." –Puritan Thomas Watson, *All Things for Good*[xxvii]

Lesson 9

The Fourth Commandment of Chivalry: You shall love your country

Bible Reading

Jeremiah 29:7

1 Peter 2:17

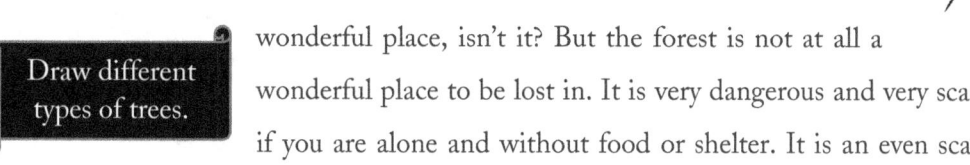

Have you ever been to the **woods** to hike or play? It's a wonderful place, isn't it? But the forest is not at all a wonderful place to be lost in. It is very dangerous and very scary if you are alone and without food or shelter. It is an even scarier place if bad men are chasing you.

> Draw different types of trees.

Guibert and Asceline felt very much alone and scared. They knew they must get as far away from Étienne and his wicked friends as they could. And so they pushed their way on through pokey **bracken** bushes, around moss-covered boulders, and past gnarled oak tree trunks. When they, at last, stopped running and slowed down—first to a walk, then to a standstill—they looked around and realized how very unfamiliar the trees around them were. They were thoroughly lost. Asceline had ridden through the lands around her father's castle for years but had not been in this particular section of the forest more than once or twice, and as twilight started to color the forest in long **shadows**, everything looked like a different world. And Guibert, of course, had never been in these thick woods so far from his homeland of Ghent.

"Guibert! I don't recognize this part of the woods!" Asceline cried. "However will we get back to the castle?"

"You've no idea which way it is?" Guibert's voice **quivered**.

"No idea at all."

"Should we go back the way we came?"

"I'm not entirely certain I can find the way back, can you?"

Guibert had to admit that he couldn't. He had expected to be back in the castle long before night-time, sitting before a **snug** firelight while everyone congratulated him on his bravery in helping Asceline. Now it looked like they might spend the night in the forest.

"I think we should stop. Things might look more familiar in the **daytime**. And we dare not wander much more. What if we wander back to Ètienne by mistake? He'll kill you, Guibert, and take me to marry that horrible Sir Achard Talcott! Oh, I'm so terrified!"

Guibert knew she was right. He was also terrified but tried not to show it.

But Guibert, like most boys in his time, was not as scared as you or I might have felt at being lost in the woods. In those days, boys did not have video games to play or movies to watch: so they played "explore-the-forest" much of the time (whenever they weren't playing "hit-each-other-with-wooden-swords"), and they watched wildlife in the woodlands.[11] In this way, they learned many of the important skills you need to know in order to live off the land with hardly more than a cloak and a knife. *But* there was one sense in which Guibert was more scared than you or I would have been: he knew better than you or I would the real and **deadly** dangers all around him hidden under that lovely woodland canopy.

> Draw a scary woodland bear!

Guibert knew, for instance (as he watched the shadows of twilight falling and felt the temperature drop) that **cold** was the most deadly danger they faced that night. If he and Asceline did not find shelter quickly they would be at risk of freezing to death. Asceline knew this also, and both of them decided it was time to make a shelter against the cold. A thin drizzle of rain started to fall through the branches above them, making them work faster. They found several large sticks, and leaned them up against a big **boulder**. Guibert had the idea of digging them into the soft forest floor like pikes in a palisade to keep them upright. Asceline had a rich woolen cloak that kept out water well, and they spread this over the sticks. Asceline also had the idea of covering her cloak with small branches and leaves to make the **shelter** blend more with the forest and hide it. This sheltered them surprisingly well against the drizzle and the wind, and they kept warm enough by huddling beneath it wrapped in Guibert's cloak together. They did not dare build a fire for fear that Ètienne might see it and find them. But they could feel it become **colder** and after some time both of them knew they might have to make a fire to survive. They decided to collect the sticks they would need. Guibert collected tinder and kindling, while Asceline collected bigger sticks for fuel, and piled them under their shelter to keep dry. Then the two children snuggled together under the shelter again to wait out the night.

> **The Survival Rule of 3**
>
> **A person can survive in the wilderness:**
> - 3 hours without warmth
> - 3 days without water
> - 3 weeks without food

---

[11] Girls spent time in the forest too, but spent more time in the castle learning domestic skills (sewing and stuff) and playing board games and telling stories.

Lesson 9: The Fourth Commandment of Chivalry

The Lean-to Shelter

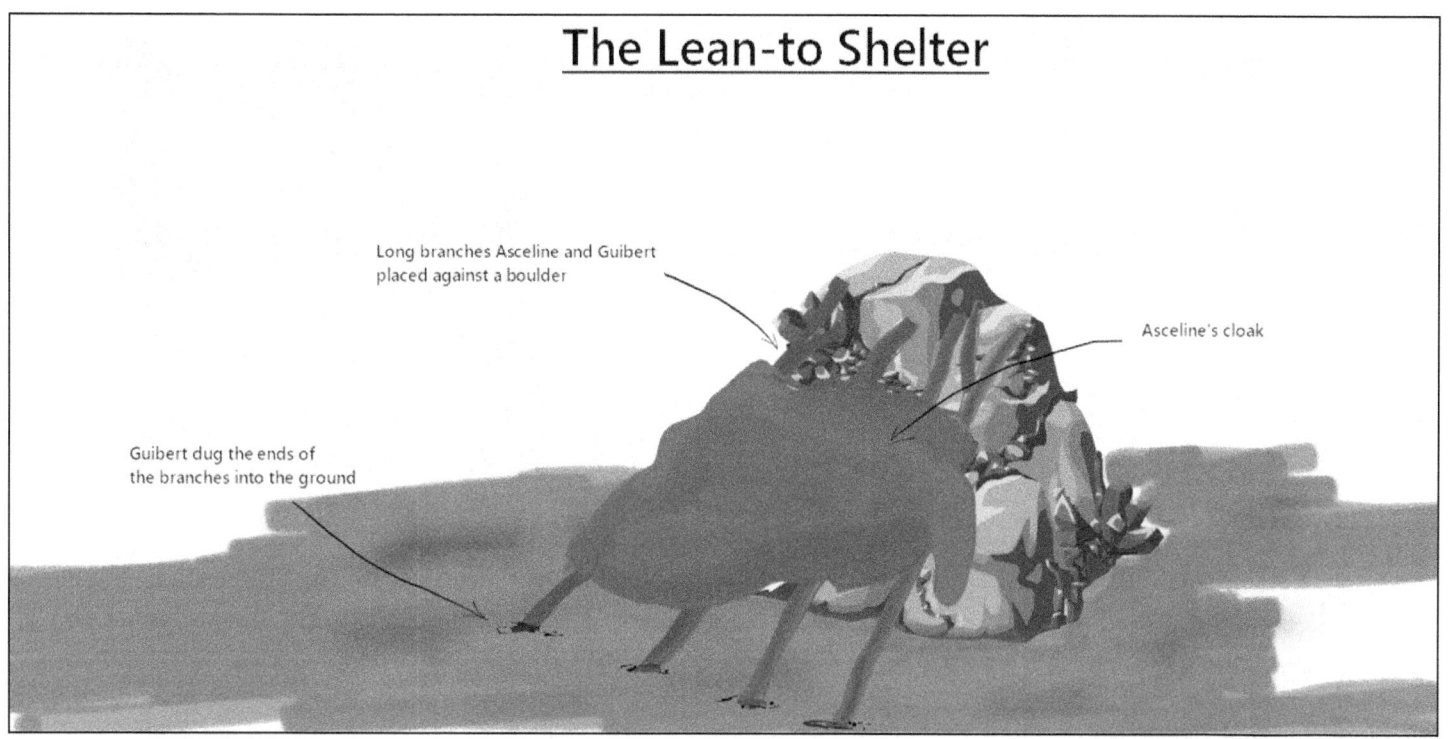

"When we failed to return I'm sure father sent out a search **party**," Asceline said, trying to be cheerful even though she was shivering. "We just have to keep away from Étienne and survive the night, so…"

AWWWWOOOOOOOOOOOOOoooooooooooooooo!!!!

The soft noise of the light rain that dripped continuously onto the forest leaves was pierced suddenly by a bone-chilling, terrible sound that made Asceline stop talking mid-sentence.

"**Wolves**!" Guibert gulped.

AWWWWWWWOOOOOOOOOOOOoooooooooooooooooo!!!!!!

"They sound far away," Asceline comforted him. She was right. But wolves can travel fast, and both children **prayed** they would not encounter any that night.

They spoke in whispers. At least they felt more prepared to weather the night. Now there was time to ask the questions that had been burning in Guibert's mind since they were treacherously attacked.

"Who is this man Étienne wishes to make you marry, Asceline?"

"Achard Talcott, lord of Haut-Loir, is his name," her voice sounded frightened at the name. "He owns a big castle and much of the land in this parts. He is old, and has an ugly **scar** over his face and horrid pouty lips! He is an enemy of my father and a greedy, vile man who would do anything for more **power**."

"Is that why he wants to marry you, for more power?" I'm sure it sounds weird to talk about a 14-year-old girl marrying a knight, but in those days rich families often married their daughters to powerful men at very young ages.

"I…I think so. Truth be told, Guibert, I'm not certain why he wants to **marry** me so badly. I *am* passing fair, but there are eligible ladies with dowers richer than mine he could have. He asked Father for a marriage alliance a month ago, and Father said no. Apparently he wants to take me by force now. Sir Talcott is constantly making friends and enemies and ever trying to get more lands. I'm surprised you haven't heard his name before now, Guibert. He is a very close friend to the Erembald family, who I think were your neighbors."

"The Erembald family!" It was Guibert's turn to speak with a tremor in his voice: a tremor of anger. "They have long been bitter **enemies** of my father, and even raided our lands once."

"Sir Achard Talcott is cousin to Bertulf FitzErembald," Asceline explained. Folk in those days knew a lot about the complicated branches in the family trees of the rich and powerful, and followed them with the same interest you or I might follow characters in a TV show or book we like.

"Bertulf FitzErembald is the biggest **scoundrel** of them all," Guibert exclaimed "I say it out loud, priest though he is. My father thinks Bertulf has been scheming with his family against Charles the Good!"[12]

"Well, if Ètienne does find us, Sir Talcott will use our marriage to become an even more powerful friend of the Erembalds. I would not be surprised if he had plans to snatch up lands in **Flanders** too." She sounded as gloomy as the rain drizzling down around them.

Guibert felt gloomy too. Flanders was the county his homeland Ghent was part of. He loved the lands he was born in. He loved their lush water-meadows and green forests and flowing rivers. He loved the busy city of Ghent and was proud of its thriving trade in wool and its famous church of St. Bravo. He was proud that his father and his father's fathers had owned the land for so long. He was proud of the Count of Flanders, who was famous for being a good man. The thought of wicked knights plotting against his homeland made his stomach churn. Now he knew more than ever that he would do anything he could to help Asceline escape the clutches of this evil Sir Talcott!

"Shhhh!" Asceline **whispered** hoarsely.

---

[12] Count Charles "the Good" ruled the county of Flanders from 1084 to 1127. Sadly, Guibert's father was right in suspecting the Erembald family of plotting against him. On March 2, 1127 they murdered Charles while he prayed in a church. The vacant countship was filled by an invader from the county of Normandy named William Clito. Sir Talcott is a pretend character, but it would be easy to imagine him plotting to help the Erembalds and William Clito.

Lesson 9: The Fourth Commandment of Chivalry

Guibert heard a sound. It was a soft sound, but it rang out over the gentle fall of the rain and the howl of the wolves like a trumpet to his ears. It was the sound of footsteps crunching wet leaves and sticks.

Guibert peeked carefully out of the shelter and pulled his head back in right away. It was Ètienne and his two thugs!

Lesson 9: The Fourth Commandment of Chivalry

Think about it, talk about it

What are some differences between Guibert's country and your country? *
_____
_____
_____

How did Guibert show he cared about his native land in this story? *
_____
_____
_____

Should we be interested in the political issues of our country?
_____
_____
_____

Dust off your quill crayon

Quest of the Day

Heraldry is not the study of a guy named Harold. No, heraldry is a complicated art invented in the times of knights, to make special symbols for each knight and his family. There are many rules of heraldry, and there are still many families and cities that have an official symbol (called a "coat of arms") today. Look over the two posters and then make your own coat of arms. (You can find downloadable color versions on my website.).

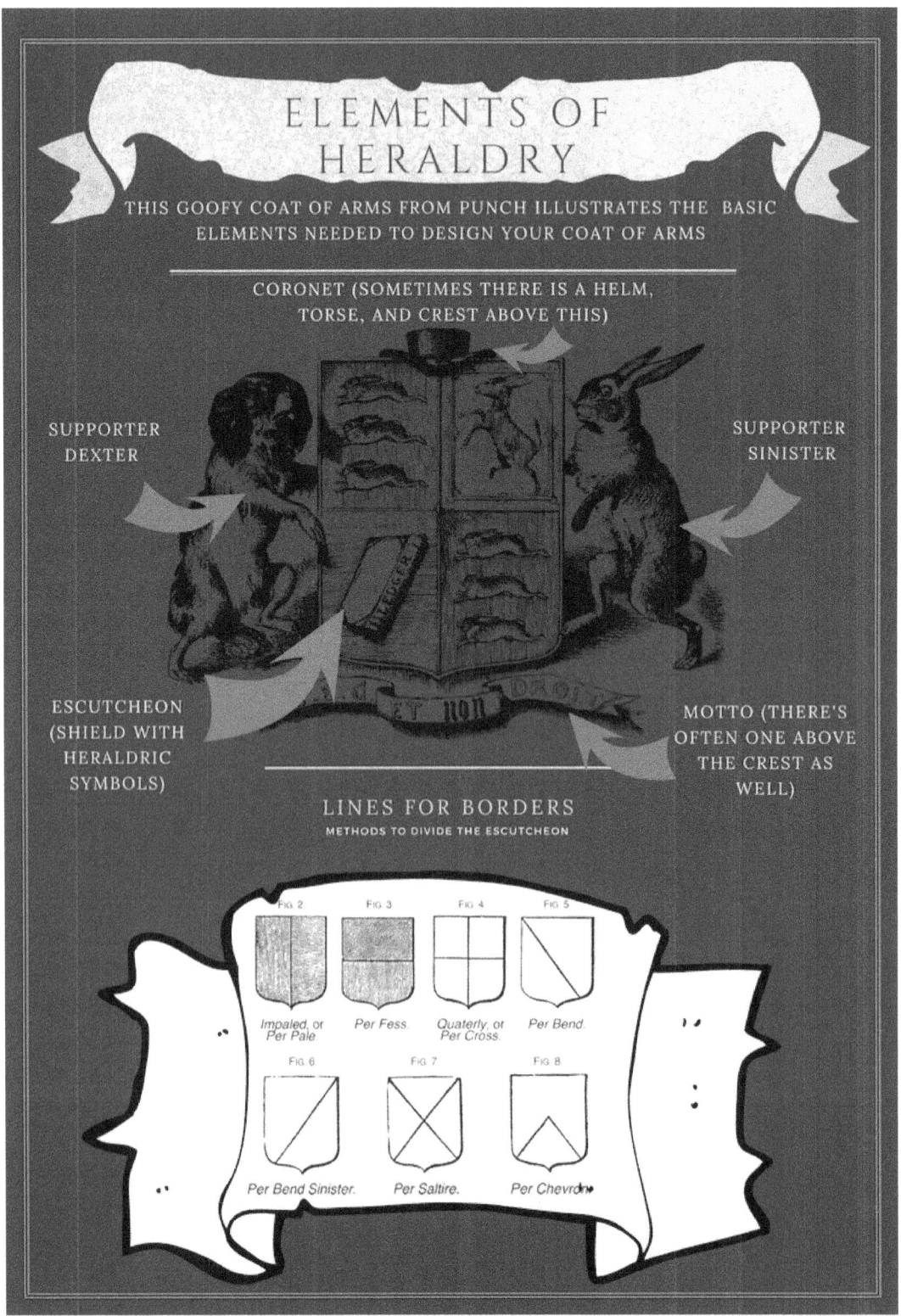

SYMBOLS OF HERALDRY
A SELECTION

BOAR'S HEAD
Hospitality

STAG
Purity and Solitude

HORN
Strength and Fortitude

BULL
Bravery and Magnanimity

CASTLE
Protection

COCK
Heroism

EAGLE
Man of action

FISH
Generosity

GRIFFIN
Valor

GOAT
Soldier
GRAPES
Peace and Liberty

KEY
Authority

SNAIL
Steadfastness and Deliberation

LION
Courage and Majesty

UNICORN
Extreme courage

RAM
Leadership and Strength

HORSE
Battle readiness

SWAN
Learning
Grace
Light and Love

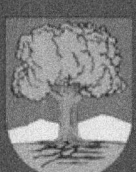
OAK
Age and strength

STORK
Filial gratitude
Vigilence (when holding a rock)

BEAR
Cunning
Ferocity
Protecting kin

COLORS

 **GOLD**
Generosity

 SILVER/ARGENT
Sincerity or Peace

 RED
Magnaminity
Strength
Martyrdom

 BLUE
Loyalty
Truth

 GREEN
Joy
Hope

 PURPLE
Majesty
Justice

 BLACK
Constancy
Grief

 ORANGE/TAWNY
Laudable ambition

Memory Verse

"But our citizenship is in heaven, and from it we await a Savior, the Lord Jesus Christ." –Philippians 3:20

Quotes

"Every good citizen makes his country's honor his own, and cherishes it not only as precious but as sacred. He is willing to risk his life in its defence and is conscious that he gains protection while he gives it." –Andrew Jackson[xxviii]

"We shall go on to the end, we shall fight in France, we shall fight on the seas and oceans, we shall fight with growing confidence and growing strength in the air, we shall defend our island, whatever the cost may be, we shall fight on the beaches, we shall fight on the landing grounds, we shall fight in the fields and in the streets, we shall fight in the hills; we shall never surrender." –Winston Churchill (4 June 1940)[xxix]

"Such is the patriot's boast, where'er we roam,
His first, best country ever is, at home."
–Oliver Goldsmith, "The Traveller" 1764[xxx]

"You who have been marked with the cross of the Christian faith, be mindful of the loyalty you owe to your fatherland and to your fellow-countrymen! If they are slaughtered as a result of this treacherous behavior by the pagans, they will be an everlasting reproach to you, unless in the meanwhile you do your utmost to defend them! Fight for your fatherland, and if you are killed suffer death willingly for your country's sake." –Geoffrey of Monmouth, 12th century, penning a battle address of King Arthur[xxxi]

Lesson 10

Your Country

Bible Reading

1 Timothy 2:1-2

Romans 13:1

The Fourth Commandment of **Chivalry** tells us, "You shall love your country." Are you proud of the country you live in? Are you proud of the lands you were born in? We might love something about the actual land in our country: the beautiful mountains it has, or the lovely **beaches** we can visit, for example. We might also be proud of men and women in our country's past and their legacy (a fancy, grown-up word for the example they left for us). God decided what country you would be born in, and He did it for a reason. He tells us in the Bible to honor the rulers of the land we live in (1 Peter 2:17), to obey the laws (Romans 13:1-5), and to try to make the **country** a better place.

> Draw a picture of your country's flag.

Loving your country is called **patriotism**. Patriotism is an important part of chivalry because it helps us respect and serve the people around us in the country where we live. It can be a noble and beautiful thing to love and to serve your country.

Are there things about your country you don't love or are ashamed of? That's OK. You can still find something to love about your country, and you can work hard, as you find opportunities, to make it a better place.

The Middle Ages

In Guibert's day, people didn't have countries as we do. They had duchies and hundreds and counties and fiefs. But loving the land you were born in (and the land you lived in) was a big part of the code of knighthood. For a knight, this meant loving his castle and the lands around it, and being **loyal** to his lord. It also meant loving his family history and being proud of his ancestors.

Your Other Country

As a Christian, you should always remember you will someday live eternally in the most wonderful land of all. That land is heaven: where there is no sadness and no badness, where we will see God himself and be **happy** with Jesus forever. Your whole life is like a road trip through this world. You will spend time in your country (or countries) just to get to your real home in **heaven**. We should always be careful not to let our patriotism, the love we have for our country on earth, make us forget the longing we have to be at last in our country of Heaven.

Lesson 10: Your Country

Think about it, talk about it

Do you know the name of your city, your county, your state, and your country? Who is the count of your county (in our days this is the governor of your state and leader of your country)?

_____
_____
_____

What are some things you can do to show you love your country?

_____
_____
_____

Who is your favorite person to read about in your country's history?

_____
_____
_____

Dust off your quill crayon

Here's a picture of the national bird (a bald eagle) and the flag of the country where I'm from. Can you color it with the right colors?

Lesson 10: Your Country

Quest of the Day

Find a favorite historical hero from your country and write about him or her. Find out and write down at least these things about them.

Name of person:
_____
_____

Date of their life:
_____
_____

What they are most famous for:
_____
_____

How they showed a chivalric love for their land:
_____
_____

Did they have a pet:
_____
_____

Why you like them:
_____
_____
_____

Quotes

"If we love our country, we should also love our countrymen." –President Ronald Reagan[xxxii]

"Patriotism is the opposite of selfish individualism." –David Ehrenfeld, *Becoming Good Ancestors*[xxxiii]

"On this green bank, by this soft stream,
We set today a votive stone;
That memory may their deed redeem,
When, like our sires, our sons are gone."
–Ralph Waldo Emerson[xxxiv]

Lesson 11

The Fifth Commandment of Chivalry: You shall not recoil before the enemy

Bible Reading

Proverbs 28:1

Deuteronomy 31:6

They are going to find us!

Young Guibert's heart pounded like a cornered rabbit's heart. He listened to the thud of three pairs of boots on the wet forest floor. His hand shook as it crept to the little dagger at his belt.

Then came a noise that changed everything.

AAAAAAArrrrrrrrroooOOOOO!!!!!

The sound was so close and so very **loud** it made Guibert and Asceline jump—even though they were trying to keep as still as possible. It sounded so wild and feral and deadly that both children shook with terror.

"**Wolves**!" the voice of one of Ètienne's thugs croaked out. "An' they sound uncommon close!"

"Get hold of your nerves," Ètienne sneered. "If we go to Haut-Loir without the girl those wolves will look friendly compared to Sir Talcott. Keep searching! They must be close."

"Juvament! The wolves round these parts be fierce, I've heered said. An' we ain't even got no horses!" The mousy-voiced villain whined. This is a good reminder for you to keep studying **grammar**, lest you grow up to be a bad guy who uses terrible grammar. Guibert noticed how unchivalrous these villains were, not once showing concern for anyone else's safety other than their own.

"Wolves killed Brom the Miller last month, an' et a **vagabond** the month before…"

A furious crashing through the brush and the padding of dozens of paws suddenly sounded in the forest on Guibert's left hand.

"By the Rood!" one of the men swore in a hoarse whisper.

"Tha's it! Oi ain't gonner be split open by wolves!" The sound of footfalls faded into the night, as the men ran off into the woods.

"Get back here, you cowardly…" Ètienne started to shout. "Um…" The

sound of the wolf pack was growing closer. The boot-falls of Ètienne faded into the night as he **ran off** into the woods away from the approaching beasts.

Both children lay still, panting with fright. They listened in terror to the rustling bushes. The sound started to come from the forest on the other side of them now.

"What should we do?" Asceline whispered hoarsely.

Guibert sat up and started stacking tinder and kindling into a pile as quick as he could. He remembered his father telling him once that wolves hate fire. His fumbling fingers bent the small **tinder** into triangles and stacked it, then he made a teepee of kindling. Lastly, he built dry fuel over all of it. He pulled out the piece of flint that he always carried in the pocket of his tunic, and struck it furiously against the steel of his dagger blade. Hot sparks flew forward but were infuriatingly reluctant to light the damp tinder.

Huff! Huff! Huff! The sound of heavy breathing was audible in the woods around them now, punctuated by excited **yips** and **barks**.

Scratch! Scratch! Scratch! Guibert struck the steel again and again until at last a tiny red glow caught among the tinder. He bent down and blew gently on the flame to expand it…

"Be…still…Guibert…" Asceline whispered, placing a warning hand on his shoulder. He looked up. A few yards away from he saw a sight that chilled him to the bone.

It was a wolf. A massive gray, **shaggy**, ragged beast of a wolf—standing full as tall as Guibert's shoulders. It growled low and menacing at them and raised its lips to show rows of jagged, bone-crushing **teeth**. Shadows moved in the dark forest behind it.

The children knew it was a foolish thing to turn and run away from a wolf once it knew you were there. Wolves are always faster than people and are more likely to chase fleeing prey. And so they stared at the beast and backed slowly away as far as possible until they were against the boulder and could go no farther. Guibert held his **dagger** in one hand and noticed Asceline pull out a dagger from within the folds of her dress. He eyed the wolf. Its hairs tingled on its back and the muscles rippled in its shoulders, ready to spring those rows of teeth upon its prey. Guibert wondered why he could see so many details in the dark night, then realized the fire he'd kindled had spread to catch the stack of dry fuel. It was flickering into a ruddy light that pierced the night. The wolf eyed the fire suspiciously, hesitating. Suddenly, the beast reared back its head and let off a spine-tingling howl into the chill night air.

AAAAAAAWWWWwwwwwwoooooooooooooo!!!!!

It was calling to its pack.

Lesson 11: The Fifth Commandment of Chivalry

A minute later, Guibert and Asceline could see the shapes of at least ten wolves pacing about them in the shadows beyond the growing firelight between the poles of their flimsy shelter. The **animals** were scared of the fire and keeping their distance, but only for a moment. They were starting to circle in closer, their teeth barred and a look of hunger in their eyes.

Guibert **gulped** down his fear, picked up a burning stick from the fire in his left hand, tightened his grip on the dagger in his right hand, and stepped up bravely to defend the entrance of their little lean-to...

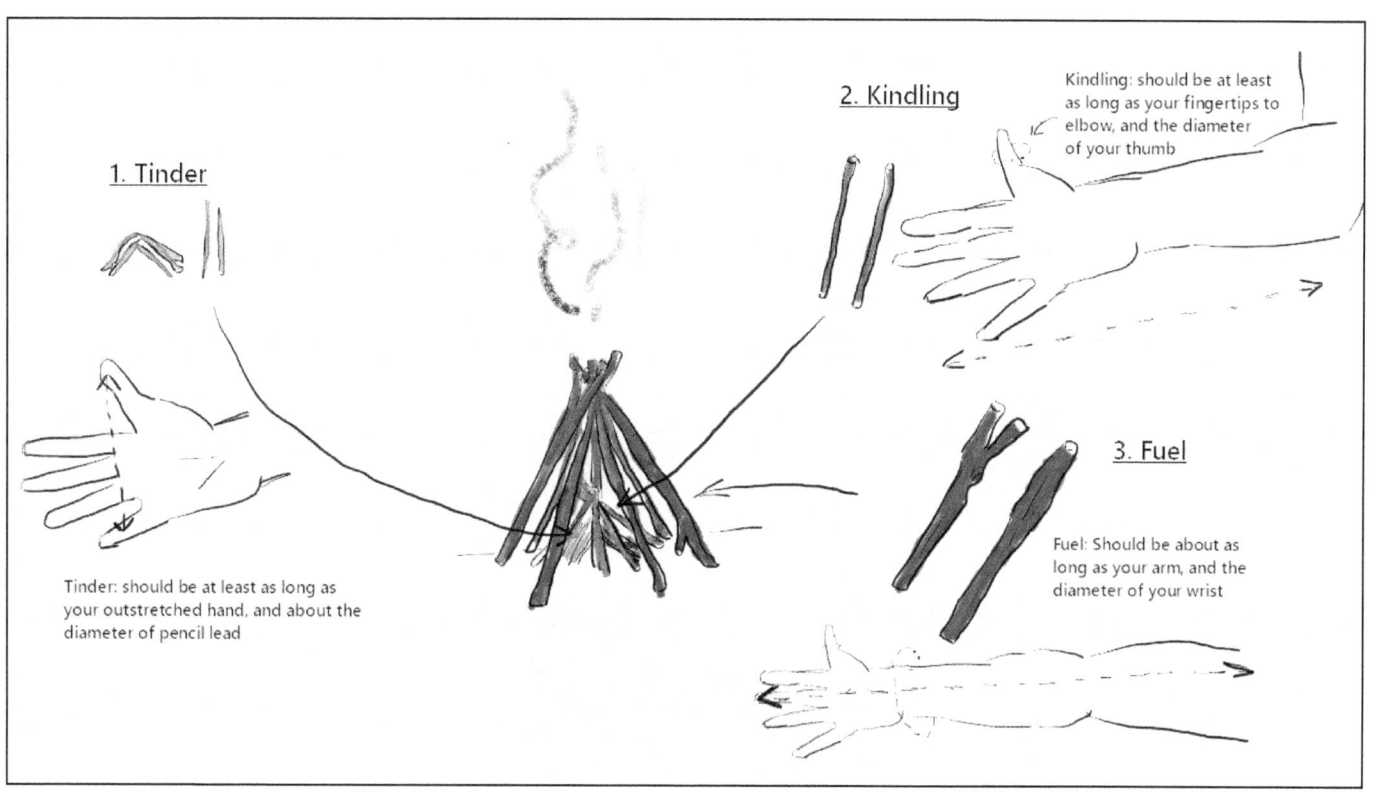

Think about it, talk about it

Do you think Guibert woke up in the morning feeling brave and ready to face a traitorous adult and fight off a pack of wolves?

___

Was Guibert afraid while he fought off the wolves? Would you have been?

___

How do you think Guibert's use of bravery to help Asceline was more chivalrous than if he had just been defending himself? *

___

Lesson 11: The Fifth Commandment of Chivalry

Dust off your quill crayon

Here are some braves knights from stories named Roland and Oliver and their lord, Charlemagne. Color them!

The Emperor sits in an orchard wide, Roland and Oliver by his side.

Quest of the Day

What do you think the knights on the previous page you just colored are brave for? Make up a story to write about one or more of them, showing some ways they are courageous. To make a good story, you will need to imagine and write about several things:

1. the theme of the story—in this case, it should be about courage (hardihood, fortitude, bravery)
2. the hero, or main character—name him and describe him
3. the battle—some problem or difficulty the character will face
4. the bad guy—may not have to be a guy. It could even be a dragon or something. But the hero will need somebody or something to fight to show his courage
5. the end—show what happened because the knight was courageous

Memory Verse

"But in your hearts honor Christ the Lord as holy, always being prepared to make a defense to anyone who asks you for a reason for the hope that is in you; yet do it with gentleness and respect." –1 Peter 3:15

Quotes

"Courage is being scared to death, but saddling up anyway." –John Wayne[xxxv]

"What makes the muskrat guard his musk? *Courage!*" –the Cowardly Lion, from *Wizard of Oz*[xxxvi]

"God, may He be thanked for it, has since I am a knight done me great good all my days; my courage now rests upon the certainty that He will continue." –William Marshal, 12th century[xxxvii]

"Being deeply loved by someone gives you strength, while loving someone deeply gives you courage." –Lao Tzu[xxxviii]

"For this is what it means to be a king: to be first in every desperate attack and last in every desperate retreat, and when there's hunger in the land (as must be now and then in bad years) to wear finer clothes and laugh louder over a scantier meal than any man in your land." –King Lune (C.S. Lewis, *The Horse and His Boy*)[xxxix]

Lesson 12

Courage and Bravery

Bible Reading

1 Corinthians 16:13

John 14:27

Have you ever felt **scared**? It's not fun, is it? Sometimes we are too afraid to do the things we need to do. And that's exactly why courage is a super important part of the Commandments of Chivalry. It takes bravery to move beyond talking about chivalry and actually do acts of chivalry outside of our comfort zones. That's why courage is the **backbone** of chivalry.

The Fifth Commandment of Chivalry tells us to "not recoil before the enemy." Recoil is a grown-up word for "run away." The type of courage that can keep a person from turning away from the enemy in battle has three important parts.

Hardihood. Hardihood means being **strong** and tough. Chivalry does teach knights to be strong. Trying to train your body and make it strong enough to do the work called for by the Commandments of Chivalry is important. This does not mean physically weak people cannot be courageous. But it does mean that we should try to keep ourselves in the best condition we can to do God's work.

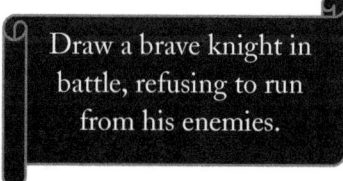

Draw a brave knight in battle, refusing to run from his enemies.

Fortitude. Fortitude is being **persistent** and stubborn, keeping on in a task even when it's hard. Chivalrous boys and girls have the willpower to move past feelings of fear and sleepiness long enough to do great things. You show fortitude when you refuse to give up. Another way you show fortitude is by staying cheerful even when a job is hard. The Bible says we should "do all things without grumbling or disputing" (Philippians 2:14). A chivalrous boy or girl does not complain or whine.

Bravery. I suspect you know what bravery is. But it may surprise you to hear that bravery is not the **absence** of scared feelings inside of you. Bravery is going ahead with something you need to do or should do, *even though* you feel scared.

The chivalrous kind of bravery is used for a good cause. It is not bravery just to prove you're tough. Knights in the Middle Ages (especially the early parts) often loved bravery just because it made a warrior look tough, even when it was used for mean things or dumb things that were needlessly dangerous. But real chivalrous courage does not go out of its way just to find danger (that would be foolish) and is never used to hurt people wrongly. It is used to uphold what is right, to **help** others in their need, to **do God's good work** on earth, and to fight against evil.

Courage in Your Life

You might be surprised at the many times in your own life when you will need courage. You hopefully will never need to defend your life or the life of another person against a bad guy or fight off a raging wolf in the woods like Guibert. But you will still need hardihood, fortitude, and bravery every day. You need courage to keep doing your schoolwork even when it's hard. You need courage to talk to people when you feel shy. You need courage to stand up for what is right when your friends want you to do something bad. You need courage to read your Bible every day and go to church every week even when you don't feel like it. You need courage to obey your parents when you **don't want to**. Sometimes you need courage just to get out of bed and go through the day.

Getting Courage

How do we become courageous? In many ways, courage is an act of the will. That means you have to **decide** to be courageous instead of **cowardly**. You get courage in a hard time by purposefully ignoring the part of you that is afraid or tired or weak, and going ahead to do what you need to do. Reading about brave men and women in the past is a good way to help you think courageously. Collecting quotes on courage helps also. Pray to God for more courage. Remember that God is on our side and that, because He's forgiven our sins already, we don't need to be afraid of **anything**.

"What then shall we say to these things? If God is for us, who can be against us?" (Romans 8:31).

Try to build chivalric courage in your life. There's almost no limit to what you might accomplish if you can conquer your fears and build up fortitude. Become brave as a lion, hardy as a rhino, and persistent as a **bull-dog**! Put that bravery, hardihood, and fortitude to work serving others through chivalry!

Lesson 12: Courage and Bravery

Think about it, talk about it

Can bravery ever be wrong? What might bad bravery look like? *
___
___
___

Can you think of a time you were scared to do something but did it anyway?
___
___
___

Is there something you should do, but are afraid to do? How can you become courageous enough to do it?
___
___
___

Lesson 12: Courage and Bravery

Dust off your quill crayon

David, though he was only a boy, showed courage in facing a gigantic warrior the grown men in the army of Israel were afraid to fight! Do you remember the giant's name? Read 1 Samuel 17. Here's a picture of David facing his foe, sketched in 1655 by a famous artist called Rembrandt. Can you trace it *and* color it?

Quest of the Day

Can you unscramble these puzzling words? (Answer in Appendix A.)

REVAB   _ _ _ _ _

SELVWO   _ _ _ _ _ _

GRONTS   _ _ _ _ _ _

NEDDEF   _ _ _ _ _ _

Quotes

"Courage is fear holding on a minute longer." –General George S. Patton[xl]

"Courage is contagious. When a brave man takes a stand, the spines of others are often stiffened." –Billy Graham[xli]

"Never bend your head. Always hold it high. Look the world straight in the eye." –Hellen Keller[xlii]

"He was an idealist who went after the attainable; a dreamer who was a man among strong men." –W.B. Hargrave, writing about Jack London[xliii]

Lesson 13

The Sixth Commandment of Chivalry: You shall make ceaseless war against the enemies of Truth, and relentlessly work to take the gates of hell by storm.

Bible Reading
1 Timothy 6:12
Romans 13:11-12

GROWL!!!! SNAP! RRRAAAGH!!!! A wolf plunged its head right through the **flimsy sticks** of the lean-to shelter and snapped its raging jaws at the two children inside.

Asceline screamed and slashed at its nose with her knife, making the wolf yelp aloud.

Guibert shouted like a crazy person and swung his firebrand at another wolf, which lunged suddenly toward the entrance to the shelter. Both wolves retreated. They continued to circle the children, however. Guibert knew it would be a matter of minutes before the **pack** was ready to charge. They could crash right through the lean-to, which meant the children would be attacked from every side but the boulder they stood against…

The boulder! Guibert looked up, a sudden idea springing to his mind. "We have to get atop this boulder!" he shouted to Asceline. He knelt and offered her his small shoulder. "Step up on my shoulder, and use the lean-to sticks to pull yourself up."

> Draw a wild boar trotting through the woods.

Asceline hesitated a moment as the wolves **circled** closer. But she saw how smart an idea it would be to get up higher, and stepped up quickly. Guibert was a tough boy, and she was a light girl. In a moment she was scrambling up the boulder's sides, pushing with her feet against the sticks of the lean-to that were tilted into the boulder's side. A snapping sound rang into the cold night, and two sticks broke in half. Her cloak fell with the broken branches, half of it right atop the fire, sending sparks everywhere. It looked a moment like Asceline would fall, but she managed to grab a handhold and scramble up on top of the boulder.

The wolves backed away from the shower of sparks for a moment. Then they seemed to realize their prey was trying to escape. Five of the beasts dashed forward with snarls and growls and bared teeth.

"Guibert!" Asceline screamed and almost jumped down to him. But then she watched amazed as the clever and **plucky** lad grabbed her burning cloak, now quite ablaze from landing on the fire, and swung it in a wide half-circle toward the wolves. He shouted as loud as he could. The sight of this little man-cub screaming like a maniac and waving fire made the wolves stop short and run back again.

But his movements had knocked down what remained of the lean-to, and Guibert had no idea how he would climb the steep **boulder,** which stood about three times taller than he was and had sides covered in

Lesson 13: The Sixth Commandment of Chivalry

slippery moss. Asceline lay down on top of the rock and stretched down her hand to him. "Your cloak, Guibert! Throw me one end of your cloak and use it like a rope!"

Brilliant! The boy quickly picked up the cloak he and Asceline had used as a blanket and threw one end to her. She caught it on the first try and held it in both hands. Guibert risked a quick glance behind him and saw the wolves moving forward again. He tugged on the cloak, **scrambling** upward. He could feel the rush of air below him and hear the snapping of doggie jaws as the wolves raged inches from his feet. He kicked furiously downward, right into the nose of one beast that jumped up at him. It yelped and fell backward, even as Guibert heaved himself over the last few inches of the boulder to lay panting on the top.

> Draw three dogs chasing your wild boar.

The wolves away again from the fire, which was spreading to the fallen branches of the broken lean-to. They paced in angry circles around the boulder. Several of them tried to scramble up the other side of the boulder. Two nearly made it but fell heavily when Asceline startled them by waving Guibert's cloak.

Both children became gradually aware of the sounds of voices in the trees nearby. In a flash, they realized their three enemies would have heard the **ruckus** of the wolf attack and seen the fire by now! Asceline trembled at the thought. Another sound came to their ears, or rather came rumbling up in a tremble that they could feel at their feet.

Horse hooves! A lot of hooves!

Five **riders** burst into the fiery glade, leveling spears at the wolves that circled the boulders. One blew a hunting horn, its clear tones ringing out across the night like the sweet song of an angel. One of them speared a big wolf full in the side, and another trampled one with his horse. A moment later, what remained of the wolf pack had vanished into the woods.

Asceline recognized all of the horseback riders. They were **servants** of her family!

"God be praised! We're rescued! We're rescued!" she wept aloud.

If Ètienne and his men had come back they never showed themselves. A broad-shouldered man with graying hair rode up to the boulder and reached out a hand.

"Come down, youngling. Your father is nearby!" Asceline hugged the man as he lifted her down, feeling happier than she ever thought she could. His name was Rollo, and he was her father's estate **steward**.[13]

"Brave lad, you are!" another man said, ruffling Guibert's wild hair after the boy had been lifted down from the boulder into the saddle in front of him. "You have a tale to tell the other pages, I'd warrant me, and no mistake!"

---

[13] A rich lord in the Middle Ages often had a guy called a steward, usually a knight, to manage the routines of his vast lands and properties. Many times there were two stewards: one to manage the lord's household schedule, and one to manage his estates.

It was true, but Guibert hardly felt like talking much just then. He was happy to be alive and wrapped in a warm new **cloak** as they rode through the cold night woodlands. In no time at all, Asceline was in her father's arms, and they were riding toward Château Bon-heur. Sir Enguerrand was angry at the children at first. But as the children told him everything, he became furious at Ètienne and Sir Talcott instead.

"The scoundrel!" he exclaimed.

"I'll suggill him with a thribble,[14] knight though he be," Rollo declared. "Just give me the word!"

Uncle Enguerrand held up a hand. "Peace, Rollo. King Henry himself shall hear of this! Or Robert's son[15] if Henry won't listen! Tomorrow I could ride to court before leaving for the **Holy Land**."

Guibert started at this. "You are leaving?"

"Yes. I was to leave upon the morrow, but now…" His words faded as he fell into brooding thought.

Guibert noticed unusual business around the marshalry (the stables where the horses were kept) when they came at last to the castle. Servants were packing carts, horses were being groomed and examined by the firelight. The blacksmith's hammer rang out, even though it was long into the dark night. A group of knights stood around a campfire in the outer bailey. They were all wearing white **surcoats** and cloaks with crosses sewn onto them.

> Draw two hunters on horses, chasing your boar with spears.

"Why is it so busy?" he asked. "Who are these new warriors?"

"I've had the servants start preparations for the morning, lad," Uncle Enguerrand said. "Several of my neighbors have taken a **crusader's** vow and are on their way to Jerusalem. King Baldwin of Jerusalem is fighting the Egyptians, and tomorrow these friends leave for the Holy Land. They asked me to join them, and I have a mind to do it."

Later that night, on his way to bed, Guibert was surprised to find the Asceline **crying** outside of her room. Little boys don't usually know what to do in situations like this, and Guibert was no different. He shuffled his feet awkwardly and coughed softly, not sure if he should give her a hug or walk away as fast as he could. She looked up with tear-stained eyes.

"Oh! Guibert! I didn't see you there. Will you come sit with me?"

He would. And he did. She put an arm around him and **sniffled**. "What are you crying for?" Guibert asked.

"I'm afraid Guibert, still afraid I shall have to marry that horrid Sir Talcott."

"But your father knows of it now. He'll keep you safe."

"But…but… He's going away, Guibert. You heard him! You saw the crusaders in the courtyard."

---

[14] Basically, "hit him over the head."
[15] This is William Clito, the same fellow plotting with the nefarious Sir Talcott and the Erembald family to take over Guibert's home of Flanders. They, along with the king of France, were enemies of King Henry I of England, whose only son and heir had died in a tragic shipwreck. William claimed the throne through his father, Robert Curthose, previous Duke of Normandy and brother to Henry. William Clito would eventually die fighting over Flanders. It's all very confusing, isn't it?

Somehow Guibert had not thought about this. He hesitated a while before he spoke. "He is going on crusade, to tear Jerusalem from the wicked hands of the Turks. My father once told me this was an honorable thing. You should be proud of him."

"I am, Guibert, I am," she burst suddenly into tears again. "And I feel wicked myself for wishing he wouldn't go. But if he does…" Her voice suddenly became a hoarse whisper and Guibert felt her trembling. "If he does go, there is little chance of him coming home."[16]

Guibert was **taken aback**— a grown-up phrase that means, "surprised and not sure what to say." He hugged Asceline and told her she wasn't wicked for wanting her daddy to stay home. A few minutes later he was on his straw bed staring up at a dark ceiling in thought. All of his short life he'd heard tales of the glorious soldiers that fought the First Crusade, and hoped to be as chivalrous as them someday in defending Christendom. But he hadn't really thought about how hard it would be for the families they left behind them. Uncle Enguerrand had a hard choice to make tonight!

---

[16] Asceline was right. Historian John France tells us that two out of every three people going on the First Crusade died. Many of these deaths would be from diseases and dangers on the road. The odds were surely not changed much for later crusades. This story takes place during the time of the Venetian Crusade, which was started by the Doge of Venice Domenico Michiel, and succeeded in growing the Kingdom of Jerusalem (the lands taken by the knights of the First Crusade) and making them safer.

Think about it, talk about it

How did Guibert defend the weak (Third Commandment of Chivalry) and show courage (Fifth Commandment) in this chapter? *

_____
_____
_____

How did Asceline defend the weak (Third Commandment) and show courage (Fifth Commandment) in this chapter? *

_____
_____
_____

What were crusaders? Do you know anything about them or the crusades? *

_____
_____
_____

Where were the crusaders Guibert met traveling to? *

_____
_____
_____

Lesson 13: The Sixth Commandment of Chivalry

Dust off your quill crayon

Color this funny picture of a chess crusader knight and a Turkish archer.

Quest of the Day

Make a crusader surcoat! A surcoat was a long, sleeveless garment a knight would wear over his armor. People vowing to go on crusades would sew a cross on their surcoat to show their promise to go to Jerusalem. Surcoats were handy to identify who was inside the armor and helmet and also to keep the hot desert sun off the armor while marching. You can make your own crusader surcoat (with the help of your mom and dad) out of an old T-Shirt by following the directions on the next page.

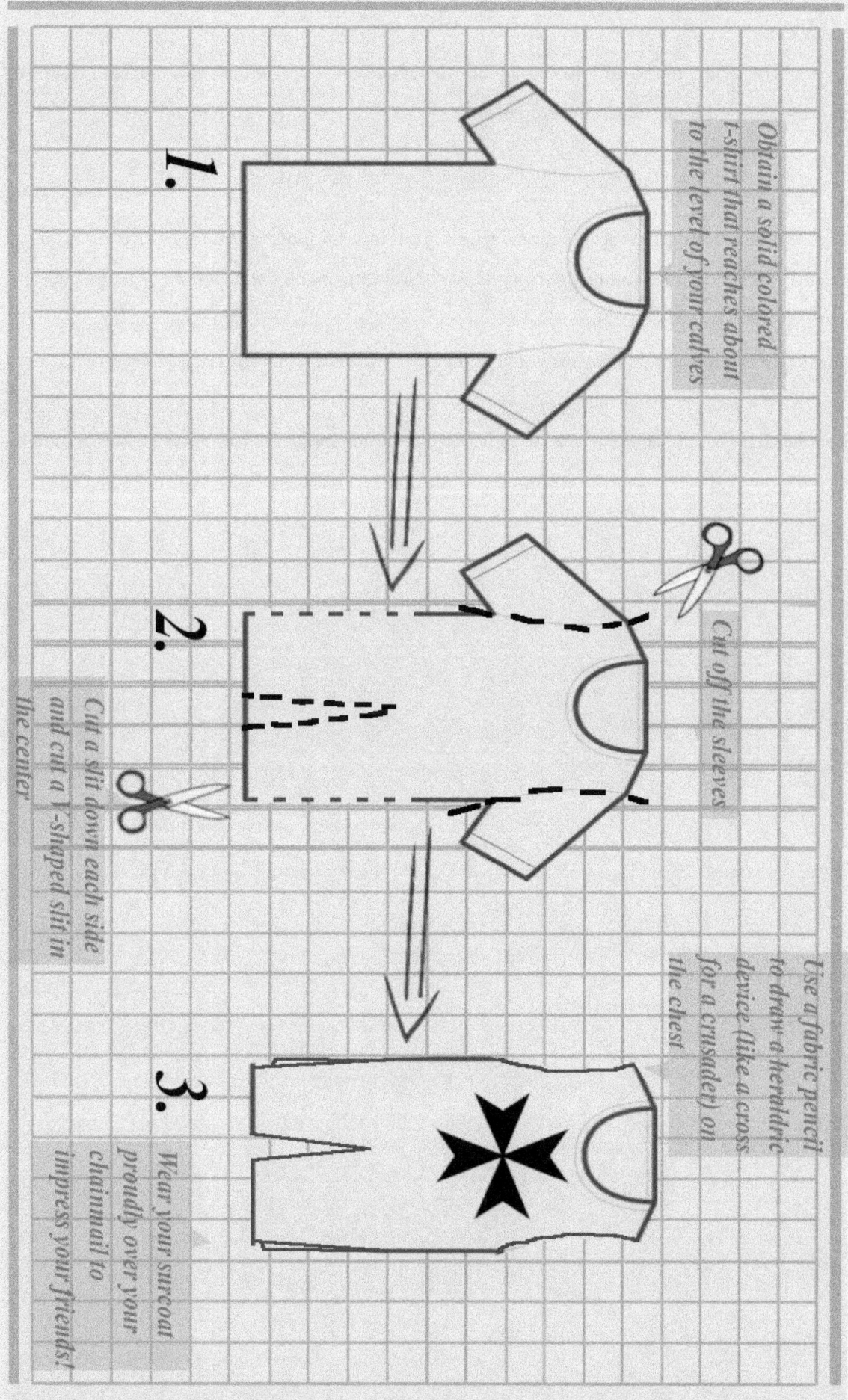

Memory Verse

"For the eyes of the LORD run to and fro throughout the whole earth, to give strong support to those whose heart is blameless toward him." –2 Chronicles 16:9a

Quotes

"If we harden our hearts and pay little attention…where is our love for God, where is our love for our neighbor?" –Bernard of Clairvaux, 12th century (writing about Islamic attacks on the Kingdom of Jerusalem)[xliv]

"What is loving God if it is not desiring his honor and glory?" –Odo of Châteauroux, 13th century[xlv]

"The true soldier fights not because he hates what is in front of him, but because he loves what is behind him." –G.K. Chesterton[xlvi]

Lesson 14

War Against God's Enemies

Bible Reading

1 Peter 5:8-9

Luke 10:19

James 4:7

The Sixth Commandment of Chivalry tells us to "make ceaseless war against the **enemies** of Truth, and relentlessly work to take the gates of hell by storm." The details of this commandment mean something different for us today than they did for knights in Guibert's day. In Guibert's day, the Sixth Commandment of Chivalry mainly meant that knights should be willing to go on the **crusades**.

Do you know what the crusades were? They were wars between armies of knights from Christian countries (like France and England), against Muslim armies in the east: especially in Jerusalem. Jerusalem, and the lands around it, are often called "The Holy Land" because Jesus walked and worked and died and rose again there when he lived on earth. To Christians in the Middle Ages, the Holy Land was especially important, and Jerusalem was the most important city in the world. Medieval people often went to the Holy Land as **pilgrims**, which means they traveled many months to pray to God in Jerusalem. Muslims worship a different god than Christians and do not believe that Jesus is God. There was a time (which Guibert's father would have remembered when he was a boy) when a Muslim people called the Seljukid **Turks** took over control of the Holy Land. The Turks hurt Christian pilgrims and attacked lands owned by other Christians called Byzantines. The Pope at the time (Urban II) preached a sermon, and asked knights to go and fight the Turks and take back Jerusalem: and they did. That was the First Crusade, and many more wars between Christians and Muslims came after it.

The vow Sir Enguerrand is thinking of taking in Guibert's story is a promise to go and fight Muslims in the Holy Land. Why do you think Sir Enguerrand would do that? There might have been many reasons. But the main reason knights at his time fought on a crusade was because they saw the Muslims as God's enemies, and thought it was their duty to fight God's enemies and keep holy places from them.

These wars were not always something God was happy with. Some of the crusaders went for bad reasons and did bad things. But many of them had a real love for

God and risked their **lives** to try and serve Him and defend other Christians from harm.

The Commandment Today

Today this Sixth Commandment means something different. God does not want us to go on a crusade or to attack His enemies with real weapons.

The Bible says in 2 Corinthians 10:4-5, "For the weapons of our warfare are not of the **flesh** but have divine power to destroy strongholds. We destroy arguments and every lofty opinion raised against the knowledge of God, and take every thought captive to obey Christ."

What chivalry demands of us today is to be ready and **willing** to tell other people about God and the truth of His Word, the Bible. A chivalrous boy or girl should have thought about why they believe the Bible, and be able to tell people why they should too.

Paul wrote in the Bible, "Fight the good fight of the faith. Take hold of the eternal life to which you were called and about which you made the good confession in the presence of many witnesses" (1 Timothy 6:12).

The main point of the Sixth Commandment of Chivalry is that Christian knights should be ready to **stand up** for Jesus whenever it's needed. It tells us to think of God's enemies as our enemies and to fight the bad things that make Him sad in this world. Christian knights should **work** to make the world a better place, and make Jesus' name great in it. We are working with Jesus on His mission in the world. He is chasing away the devil and putting away the badness the devil brings about in the world. His knights should fight with him against bad things and always be on the lookout for the **tricks** of Satan. Jesus is bringing more and more people to believe and trust Him as Savior. His knights should be trying hard to show the world how great Jesus is and to help more and more people believe in Him.

This is the time in history between when Jesus rose again, and when he will come back from Heaven to bring us all to live with Him in happiness forever. And in this time, we have the chivalrous **honor** of working with Him to make the world better in any way we can, to bring people to Him, and to chase away badness wherever we can! This is our mission. This is part of the great adventure of chivalry!

Think about it, talk about it

Do you remember reading about the difference between the ideal type of Chivalry and the history type of Chivalry in Lesson 2? What are some ways the ideal of the Sixth Commandment of Chivalry is different from its history type of chivalry for this commandment? *

What are some ways you might be called to stand up for Jesus in your life?

What are some things you can actively do now for Jesus and His kingdom?

How can you move from saying/writing them down to doing them?

Dust off your quill crayon

Quest of the Day

The word "apologetics" is a grown-up word that means "giving a reason for something you believe." Being able to tell people why you believe in the God of the Bible is an important part of what the Sixth Commandment of Chivalry means to us today.

So how about you? Do you have good reasons to believe in God, reasons you can explain to someone who asks you? Talk with your mom and dad about this and answer these two questions…

Why do you believe in God?

_____
_____
_____

Why do you believe the Bible is true?

_____
_____
_____

Quotes

"If Christianity was something we were making up, of course we could make it easier. But it is not. We cannot compete, in simplicity, with people who are inventing religions. How could we? We are dealing with Fact. Of course anyone can be simple if he has no facts to bother about." –C. S. Lewis, *Mere Christianity*[xlvii]

"Men do not reject the Bible because it contradicts itself, but because it contradicts them." –E. Paul Hovey[xlviii]

"Truth is like the sun. You can shut it out for a time, but it ain't goin' away." –Elvis Presley[xlix]

"The truth is incontrovertible. Malice may attack it, ignorance may deride it, but in the end, there it is." –Winston Churchill[l]

"Better to fight for something than live for nothing." –George S. Patton[li]

Lesson 15

The Seventh Commandment of Chivalry: You shall faithfully perform your responsibilities, and shall honor all your commitments.

Bible Reading
Colossians 3:23

"**Verily**, yes. Aye! Of a surety shall I watch your goats, Humbert! It shall be **no problem!**" Guibert jabbered merrily to his friend Humbert the gatward.

It was three days after Guibert's harrowing adventures in the woodlands, and he'd been hailed a **hero** and enjoyed some time off from his duties. His Uncle Enguerrand decided not to go on crusade, but to outfit five poorer knights and ten of his best sergeants to send in his stead. Though it was a great honor to fight for Christ with the crusaders, he told his pages and squires, it would be greater **dishonor** to leave his family and his castle when they were in danger.

> Draw a picture of your favorite flower or herb.

So now the two boys were lying on their backs atop the little shed of the goat pen. It was built in a corner where the outer bailey of Château Bon-heur joined the curtain wall of the inner bailey. Guibert had gotten in the habit of bringing food (which he saved from the leftovers of the rich castle meals) to Humbert and his family as often as he could since they were very poor and sometimes went hungry. They were munching on bits of dried honeycomb Guibert had got from the kitchen as they peered up into a cold night sky **ablaze** with stars. It was a peaceful and pleasant way to relax with a friend after a long day of page duties. It was the kind of night you could make all sorts of promises comfortably.

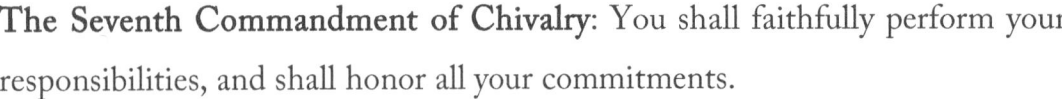

"Are you sure, Guibert?" Humbert sounded a bit skeptical. "There be a powerful lot of goats in the pen now: a billy goat and a wether, seven does and two nanny goats milking, and a full half score kids, all still a-nursing. They'll need new hay twice a day and a cup of grain and…"

Guibert held up a hand. "Nay, nay. I can do it. My only big task tomorrow is to deliver a message for Dame Blanche, the cook's wife. She noticed tonight that an outflow drain at the keep near the kitchen had eroded enough to let little **goblins** and satyrs[17] into the castle. She's ever the one to be frightened by such silly things! Haha! She gave me the job of bringing a message to the castle

---

[17] A satyr was a half-goat half-man creature in mythology. Medieval people thought of them as bad and devilish.

mason to fix the drain. I suppose I should have done it at once, but wanted to visit with you, so I must do it early tomorrow. But it can wait until the goats are fed. I want to see the knighting of the two squires Jean and Chrétien but that's not 'til later in the day. Nay Humbert, 'twill be **no problem!**" he said again.

"Then let me show you how to feed them and how the gate—"

Guibert raised a hand again for silence. "Nay! I don't need you to teach me how to feed a few goats."

Humbert shrugged. "Many thanks, Guibert. My poor sister's got her a fever with teething. Since we cannot afford to pay an apothecary, mother's asked me to go into the woods and find as much celandine as I can for her **sore** mouth, and betony to help her sleep. It doesn't grow nearby, and I'll probably miss the knighting. But poor Bernice needs something."

They were quiet for a moment as they gazed at the stars. "Look!" Humbert exclaimed, pointing above them. "I can see Boötes with his club! I wonder if'n them two squires see him tonight too. An old warrior runnin' about after heavenly bears might inspire them as they enter knighthood."[18]

Guibert cast a puzzled look at his friend and wondered how the connections in a gatward's brain worked. "I doubt it. They are supposed to be **praying** all night in vigil at the chapel, to prepare themselves before God for knighthood."

"What? All night! Zounds! I could never pray all night long," said Humbert.

"I suppose that's why a gatward's never become a knight," Guibert smiled.

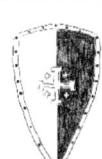

Though he already had two tasks to do that morning, Guibert slept in and set out late. He started his day with the near-forgotten job of feeding **goats**. It was a frosty morn with a chill wind. Zwane didn't seem to like this at all, and wriggled and rolled in his master's pocket to find the warmest corner. Guibert focused on holding the woolen cloak about his neck with one hand, while he opened the gate with his other hand.

"This will be **no problem**…" he muttered to himself through chattering teeth.

"Ribbit!" shouted Zwane, as if to say "Yipes! Zounds and Juvament! Get me away from here!" He leaped out of Guibert's pocket.

"Hey! Come back here," Guibert caught the toad and stuffed him into his pocket again. But he turned so quickly to do it that he accidentally kicked over the bucket of oats that sat outside the gate.

---

[18] Boötes is a constellation (a picture in the stars) that medieval people wrote about. The story goes Boötes follows other constellations called Ursa Major and Ursa Minor (little and big bears) with a club in his hand. Arcturus, the brightest star in the constellation, means "guardian of the bears."

"MMAAAAAAAaaaaaaa!!!!!!!!!!!"

The screams of the 21 goats roared out frantically. Their odd, rectangular pupils widened at the site of the delicious **oats** all over the ground. 84 hooved feet dashed toward the open gate.

> Draw a goat, then draw another goat...then draw 19 more goats.

"Ack!" Guibert grunted as the first four goats shoved into him to nibble with busy lips at the oats on the cold ground. He waved his arms to stop the rest. He managed to slam the gate shut before more could escape.

"This is...er...**no problem**..." he muttered dubiously, wondering how to put the escaped goats back into the pen without letting the others out. He would just have to lift them over the fence one by one.

"Erg...." One page boy's muscles strained, one set of goat legs flailed, and—thump!—one goat fell over the fence and into the pen.

"Oof!" Another goat over.

"Arg!" The third goat had the advantage of knowing Guibert's **plan**, and she flailed and kicked much harder. But—thump!—she fell into the pen in the end.

The fourth goat was a clever yearling **buck**. Guibert recognized him (by the funny rat-shaped white mark on his back) as a goat Humbert had named "Ratramnus"—which Guibert had always felt was a mite disrespectful.[19] Ratramnus saw the fate of his fellow goats, took a last lingering nibble at the oats, and then trotted away with all the speed of a rabbit running from a pack of dogs.

"Oy!" Guibert cried. "Get back here, you acclumsid gandygut!"[20]

Ratramnus listened to Guibert about as well as I suspect your two-year-old brother listens to your mommy. He scampered around a wooden shed and was gone from view. Guibert ran after him but rounded the corner to find the **beast** vanished. It seemed like some dark magic.

"But how...?" he started. Then he noticed hoof prints in the wet ground near a little drain that ran through the wall between the baileys. Guibert groaned inside. He went back and made sure the gate to the goat pen was securely locked, then jogged down the dirt path to the inner bailey of Château Bon-heur.

"Ratramnus! Ratraaaaamnus!" he shouted through **cupped** hands as he ducked in between outbuildings. He dodged around bustling castle servants and peasants and workers, trying not to seem too crazy. He searched for an hour, but the ingenious little goat-kid seemed to have the superpower of invisibility. At last, he came across a clue—a small hole in the castle grist mill (the building where flour was made) chewed all around with goat teeth-marks. He

---

[19] Ratramnus of Corbie was a famous monk from Charlemagne's time.
[20] Acclumsid means "foolish" or "dumb." Gandygut means "somebody who eats too much."

couldn't fit through the little hole, so he ran to the door in front and found it open. A little trail of floury hoof prints exited the mill. They were leading toward the castle keep, where Guibert knew crowds were gathering in the great hall to see Uncle Enguerrand make squires into knights.

"This **is a problem!**" he puffed, beads of sweat starting to form on his face despite the chill air.

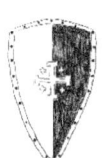

Becoming a knight was a big deal for a squire. It was so important that some knights (like a real knight named William Marshal) wrote that they felt their life began on the day they were knighted. Most of a boy's life in those days led up to that **moment** of knighthood. Some squires spent years trying to become a knight never to become one. When a squire was going to be made a knight he had to take a special **bath** that symbolized him being washed of his sins by Jesus. He dressed in white linen to symbolize his purity, then he had to lay his weapons on the altar of the chapel and spend all night long praying ("keeping vigil"). After his vigil was done, he would appear before the lord, kneel, and they would say special words. The lord would buckle on the new knight's belt and sword, and "dub him"—touch his shoulders with a sword. Jean and Chrétien (the two knights-to-be) would have been grateful that Sir Enguerrand used the newer dubbing for a knight, instead of the older "paumée"—which involved the lord **slamming** both fists into the kneeling squire's shoulder, hard enough to knock him down! After the new knight was dubbed, he went outside and dashed around on his horse to show his skills, then maybe threw some coins to poor people.

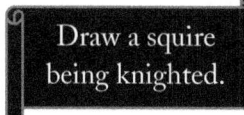

All this is very interesting to read about, but Guibert knew it already. It was part of his life. What went through his head again and again the morning of the knighting was not facts about knighting ceremonies, but the words, *That dumb goat might ruin the most important day of Jean and Chrétien's lives!*

He followed the white, ghostly trail of tiny **hoof prints** outlined in flour as it wound across the open space toward the castle keep. He was relieved to see the hoof prints led away from the pentice stairs (a roofed and walled walkway) that led directly into the Great Hall on the second story. But then the flour faded and he had to spend precious time searching for more tracks. It was getting closer to midday, and Guibert could hear drummers inside the Great Hall and voices chanting the start of the ceremony of knighthood. At last, he saw the little goatling's hoof prints indenting the soft mud around a drain pipe near the kitchen. It was the same drain in need of repair, about which he'd forgotten to take Dame Blanche's message to the mason: and it was just the right size to let a little goat into the walls of Château Bon-heur's keep![21]

---

[21] Many castle keeps in Guibert's day used a clever system of ducts for running water. There was a basin on top of the keep, where servants poured water, and a system of primitive pipes running down through the walls. Each floor had its own central sink where

"No! No! No!" the page boy murmured miserably as he tried to poke his head and shoulders through the hole to peer into the **darkness**. There was no way to climb in further. He heard a faint, echoing "maaaa!" somewhere in the darkness. He yelled at the goat to come back. The only response was the sound of clambering hooves as he frighted Ratramnus further into the keep.

Guibert jogged back to the pentice and up the steep, winding stairway into the Great Hall. Inside the people nearest the door turned and glared as he accidentally slammed it shut with an embarrassed cringe. But the rest of the crowd was too busy gazing around the hall wondering where the sudden bleating sounds were echoing from.

"Maaaaaa! Maaaaaah!!!! Meeeeeeeeeeeeh!!!!!!"

Guibert cringed again. The echoes grew **louder and louder**. Then they stopped abruptly. He could see Dame Blanche in the corner, trembling in the arms of her husband. He could see Lady Asceline, dressed in a beautiful new cloak of blue, look about the hall with a perplexed and amused grin. He could see Chrétien, dressed in white tunics, kneeling before Sir Enguerrand on the raised dais at the front of the hall. Jean was already knighted and stood nearby with a sword buckled at his hip. The one thing he could not see was Ratramnus the goat.

"Hmm…" Sir Enguerrand hesitated, then proceeded with his work of buckling a **sword** upon Chrétien. "Chrétien of Rouen, I bestow on you this sword that you might energetically exercise justice, and might overturn the triumphant edifice of iniquity…"[22]

"Mwwweeeeeeh!"

A bleeting sound rang out from the walls, but Sir Enguerrand continued with hardly a pause.

"Remember, O knight, that you are to act as the **defender** of Order and as the avenger of Injustice…"

"Maaaaaah!" the goatly sound sounded again. Guibert pushed his way through the crowds as quietly as he could and started running his hand and ear against the wall in the desperate hope of locating Ratramnus. Poor Dame Blanche could be heard muttering, "The goblins! The goblins and the satyrs!" Sir Enguerrand continued, though he sped up the words.

"'Tis on this condition…"

"Maaaaa!"

"…'tis on this condition, I say again, living here below as a copy of Christ, that…"

"Meeeeeeeeh!"

---

water could be poured out through spigots for washing or drinking. The water eventually ran out of the drain at the base of the castle. Nobody wanted to drink the water at Château Bon-heur after the goat scurried all around the drain pipes!

[22] Sir Enguerrand uses a formulae we have recorded from medieval knighting ceremonies in the Basilica of St. Peter in Rome.

Lesson 15: The Seventh Commandment of Chivalry

"…that you will reign eternally…"

"Mwaaaaaaaah!"

"… er…eternally above with…"

Creaaaaak. A soft wooden sound came from behind the big chair Sir Enguerrand usually sat in.

"Um, with your Divine Model. I now dub you a knight." Sir Enguerrand finished his words at last and raised the sword to dub Chrétien. At the same moment a silhouette resembling a goat, made **vast** and monstrous by the flickering candles and oil lamps of the dim keep, was cast behind Chrétien upon the wall.

"EEEEEEEEEEEEEEEEEEEEEEEEAAAAAAAAAAAAAAAAAAK!" Dame Blanche shrieked out loud. That was all the poor woman could take. She ran screaming from the hallway. "Satyrs! Satyrs and goblins and devils! Saints preserve us all, we're beset!"

"YAAAAAH!" Chrétien **yelled** at nearly the same moment. The poor squire unexpectedly felt something nibbling and tugging at his tunic.

Sir Enguerrand turned in astonishment: and the flat of the sword fell upon the shoulder of Ratramnus the **goat**, all pale as a ghost and covered in flour.

"Meeeeeeeh!" bleated the newly made knight, flipping his upper lip about in disapproval.

There was immediate hubbub and uproar about the hall. People screamed. People **babbled** in surprise. Asceline laughed and laughed. Guibert heard someone nearby remark, "I think a goat just came up from behind the ol' lord's chair! Is there a secret passage?"

"'Tain't no **secret** no more!" a fellow next to him chuckled.

Chrétien, when he'd recovered from his first terror, erupted in an angry, unchivalrous oath and pushed his way through the crowds to storm out of the castle.

"What in the blessed isle of Tabrobane is the meaning of this whoopubb?"[23] Sir Enguerrand roared aloud. Nearly everyone grew quiet on the instant… Except of course Sir Ratramnus, who said "Maaaaa?"

"Who let that **goat** in here?"

Guibert froze in place. He didn't move. He started forward. Then he stopped. Should he tell Sir

---

[23] Whoopubb is a fun, old word for "craziness." Tabrobane was a mythical island in medieval stories.

Enguerrand it was his neglect that had let the goat-kid into the keep? He would be in mountains of trouble if he did. And if he said nothing, nobody would know.

What to do? Oh, what to do?

Lesson 15: The Seventh Commandment of Chivalry

Think about it, talk about it

Was Guibert faithful to his friend Humbert? Was he faithful in his page boy duties to Sir Enguerrand and his household?

_____
_____
_____

What should Guibert do now? What do you think he will do?

_____
_____
_____

Has there been a time where things went wrong because you didn't do what you were supposed to do?

_____
_____
_____

Do you think castles had secret passages? Why would a castle have a secret passage? *

_____
_____
_____

Dust off your quill crayon

Folk in the Middle Ages cared a lot about the stars. They used them to navigate (find their way when traveling), tell the time and seasons, and tell stories. Now we do all this with our phones, but medieval people had to use stars. Studying the stars is called astronomy. Sometimes medieval folk used stars for superstitious reasons also and pretended to be able to tell the future through them (a bad thing called astrology). People sometimes still do this.

Medieval scholars sometimes used constellations as symbolic of Christian stories. A constellation is a group of stars that outline a picture. On the next page is a diagram on parchment written in England sometime between 800-1200 AD, and based on the scholarly works of Isadore of Seville, Abbo of Fleury, and Bede and was used by monks to help study the stars and keep track of seasons. This diagram shows the zodiac constellations arranged around the earth with the corresponding months and planetary bodies associated with them. Go outside tonight and find a real constellation. Draw it. You may need to look at a star chart or a book of constellations, such as H.A. Rey's book *The Stars*. There are some good cell phone apps to find constellations through a phone's camera as well.

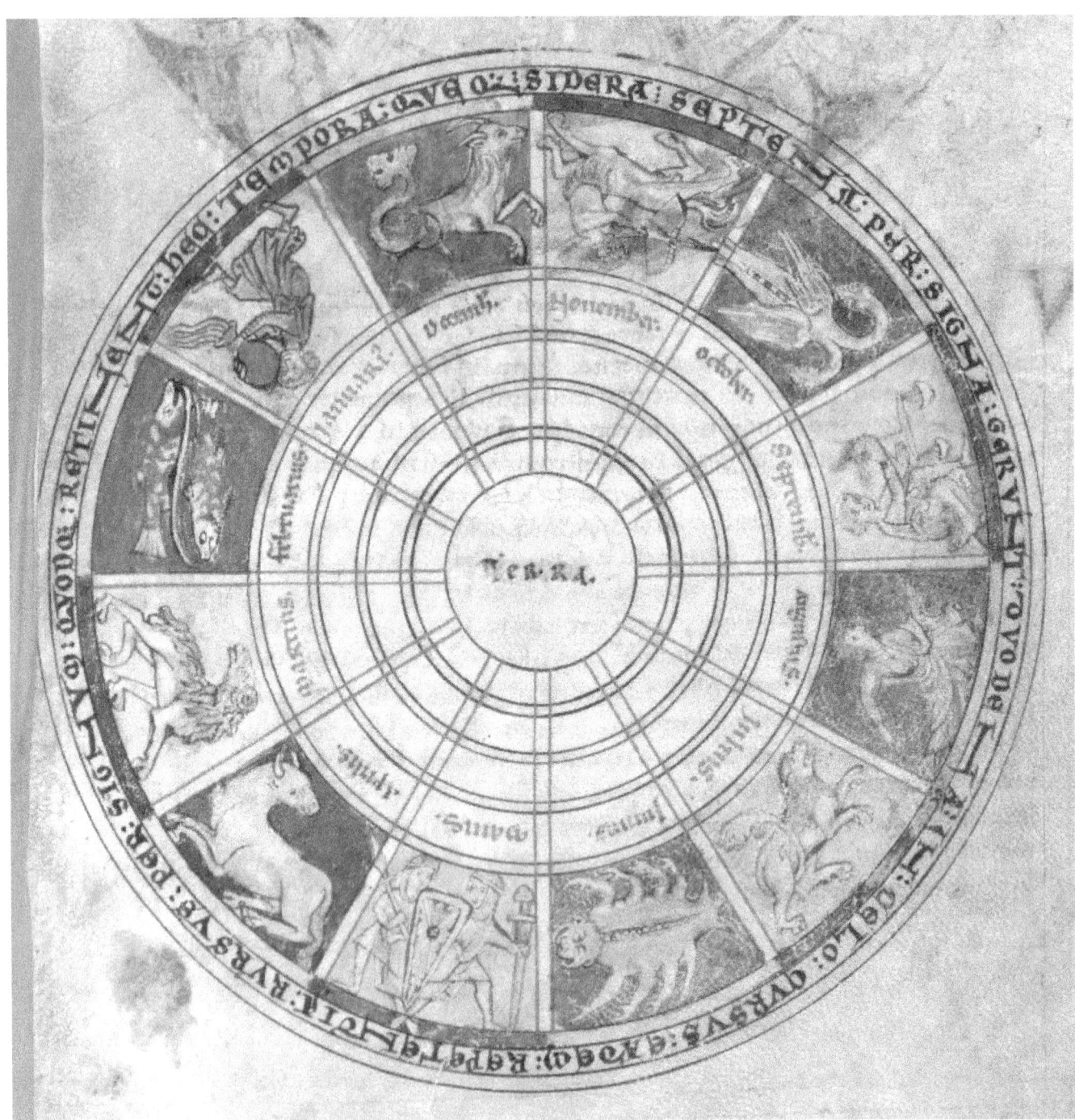

Quest of the Day

Think about someone in your life who loves you consistently and dependably fulfills a duty to you. Write them a note to say thank you and hand it to them or mail it to them.

Lesson 15: The Seventh Commandment of Chivalry

Bonus Quest!

Solveth ye this crossword puzzle post-haste! Verily and yea!

Across
4. Doing your duty all the time
5. The tap to make the knight
6. A warty friend for a pocket

Down
1. What you become when you do your duty all the time
2. Acts you owe to folks you know
3. A squire becomes one

Memory Verse

"One who is faithful in a very little is also faithful in much, and one who is dishonest in a very little is also dishonest in much." –Luke 16:10

Quotes

"Every Knight remembers (his dubbing) as the finest (day) of his existence." –George Duby[lii]

"Action springs not from thought, but from a readiness for responsibility." –Dietrich Bonhoeffer[liii]

"Happiness and moral duty are inseparably connected." –President George Washington[liv]

"Liberty means responsibility. That is why most men dread it." –George Bernard Shaw[lv]

Lesson 16

Faithfulness, Consistency, and Dependability

Bible Reading

Proverbs 18:24

Philippians 1:27

Faithfulness

For a medieval knight the Seventh Commandment of Chivalry ("You shall faithfully perform your responsibilities, and shall honor all your commitments") would mostly mean he must be true and faithful to his liege-lord. *Faithfulness* is a grown-up word that means being **true-hearted** to someone, and always doing the duty that you owe to them. Today we don't swear allegiance to the lord of a castle. Instead, we need to be faithful to a lot of other people. Did you know you owe a duty to people in your life? Relationships (that is, being a son or daughter, or a friend, or a brother or sister) bring duties and they bring things we are supposed to do for the people we **love**.

Draw yourself and your family.

Humbert the gatward showed chivalric faithfulness in his duty to his family (his mother and his sister) by giving up his whole morning to go picking **herbs** to help Bernice with her teething pains, even though he would miss the knighting ceremony. Who might you owe a duty to? A bigger word for the duty that comes with a relationship is responsibility. Who do you have a responsibility to in your life right now? Here are some responsibilities I suspect you already have at this very moment.

- Responsibility to **obey** your parents and listen to them and treat them with respect. "Children, obey your parents in the Lord, for this is right. 'Honor your father and mother' (this is the first commandment with a promise)" (Ephesians 6:1-2).
- Responsibility to be **kind** to your sister(s) or brother(s), to help them, and don't fight with them.
- Responsibility to help **keep** your little brother or sister safe.
- Responsibility to be **friendly** to your friends, to keep your promises, and not betray them.
- Responsibility to do your **chores** and your schoolwork.
- Responsibility to **respect** your grandparents.

As you get older, you will get new relationships (by making new friends, getting married, having kids), which bring whole new responsibilities. Faithfulness is being careful to always do the duties the relationships in your life demand. This is a very important part of the knight's code of chivalry. If courage is the backbone of chivalry, faithfulness is chivalry's lifeblood.

Consistency

A vital part of all this is *consistency*. Doing your duty all or most of the time is called consistency. Consistency is the **key** to the Seventh Commandment of Chivalry and one of the most important ways chivalry makes us strong men and women of God. And it is very, very hard—even for grown-ups! It's hard because many days in our lives duty can **feel** like drudgery instead of the adventure that it is. Responsibility often seems ordinary and boring to us. And sometimes doing our duty is not fun. It takes work. It can be tough and demanding and make us tired. It can be cold and long, like the job of that tower guard in the picture below (by Leo Schnug). It's easy enough to be tough and work hard for something that feels exciting and new and interesting. But it takes real strength to consistently do your duty to everyone day after day in the ordinary course of your life. And that's where it really is exciting. It's a challenge! And it's good, good **work**.

Guibert was not consistently faithful in his duty. He did a good job helping Asceline in the woods and did his page's duties regularly. But he got lazy with his job of carrying a message for Dame Blanche about the eroded drain and didn't take his promise seriously to Humbert to take care of the goats. And look what disaster came from that!

Your feelings make consistency hard. All your life you will have some days that stand out: thrilling days when you are excited to do something for someone you especially like, days you are excited to work on some new project that interests you, or see some great movie you've been waiting for. But much more of your life will be **filled up** by the boring, ordinary days—days where you have to make yourself **strong** enough to obey your parents and be kind to your siblings, days when you have to press on to finish schoolwork you're not even a little bit interested in, days you don't get to do something new or interesting but just have to slog through. But the funny thing is, when you make yourself do what's right even when you don't feel like it, you often **turn** those dull days into adventurous days. It's exciting to realize you are serving God and doing good by being consistent.

Remember that you show real chivalric strength when you **make** yourself do your jobs and your chores even on those boring days. Remember that you show real chivalric love when you do your duty to people in your life you aren't particularly excited to do it for. Love like that is love like Jesus' love: it is love that means something, it is love that people can depend on.

Dependability

Consistency makes you dependable. *Dependability* is the most important word to remember when you think of the Seventh Commandment of Chivalry. Dependability is the goal we are trying to achieve. If we want to follow the Ancient Code of Chivalry, we must above all be dependable people: people that our friends and our brothers and sisters and our mothers and fathers know will do our duty. Dependability means being faithful so people know they can rely on you. This is a very important part of life as you grow up. As you get older, and maybe get married and have kids of your own, your duties to be faithful and dependable will only grow. Now is the time in your life to build the habit of being faithful and consistent and dependable so you can serve the people you love well, for God's glory and their good. If you can do that, you will set yourself up for happier relationships and more successful work all your life. But more importantly, you will be following Jesus' great example, and living the real-life adventure of chivalry!

Think about it, talk about it

Why is it so hard to be consistent and dependable in our duty? *

_____
_____
_____

Every person has had times when they failed to do the duty they owe someone in their life. Can you think of a time you failed somebody you love? Does that mean you are not a dependable person, and should just stop trying to follow the Seventh Commandment of Chivalry?

_____
_____
_____

Does God owe us anything? How does your answer to that question make His consistent, dependable love for us so much more amazing? *

_____
_____
_____

How can being faithful, consistent, and dependable change the world for the better? *

_____
_____
_____

Lesson 16: Faithfulness, Consistency, and Dependability

Dust off your quill crayon

Color yon picture of a busy castle!

Quest of the Day

Behold the remarkable **Stairway of Dependability**! Start learning habits of faithfulness to your duty in order to become dependable. Talk to your mom and dad, and pick a chore to do (like cleaning the table after breakfast, or making your bed in the mornings, or taking out the trash). See if you can remember to do that chore every day for the next 2 weeks, and check the box on the **Stairway of Dependability** when you finish it. When you do your duty with consistency, you become a dependable knight of the Seventh Commandment of Chivalry! (There is a color version online.)

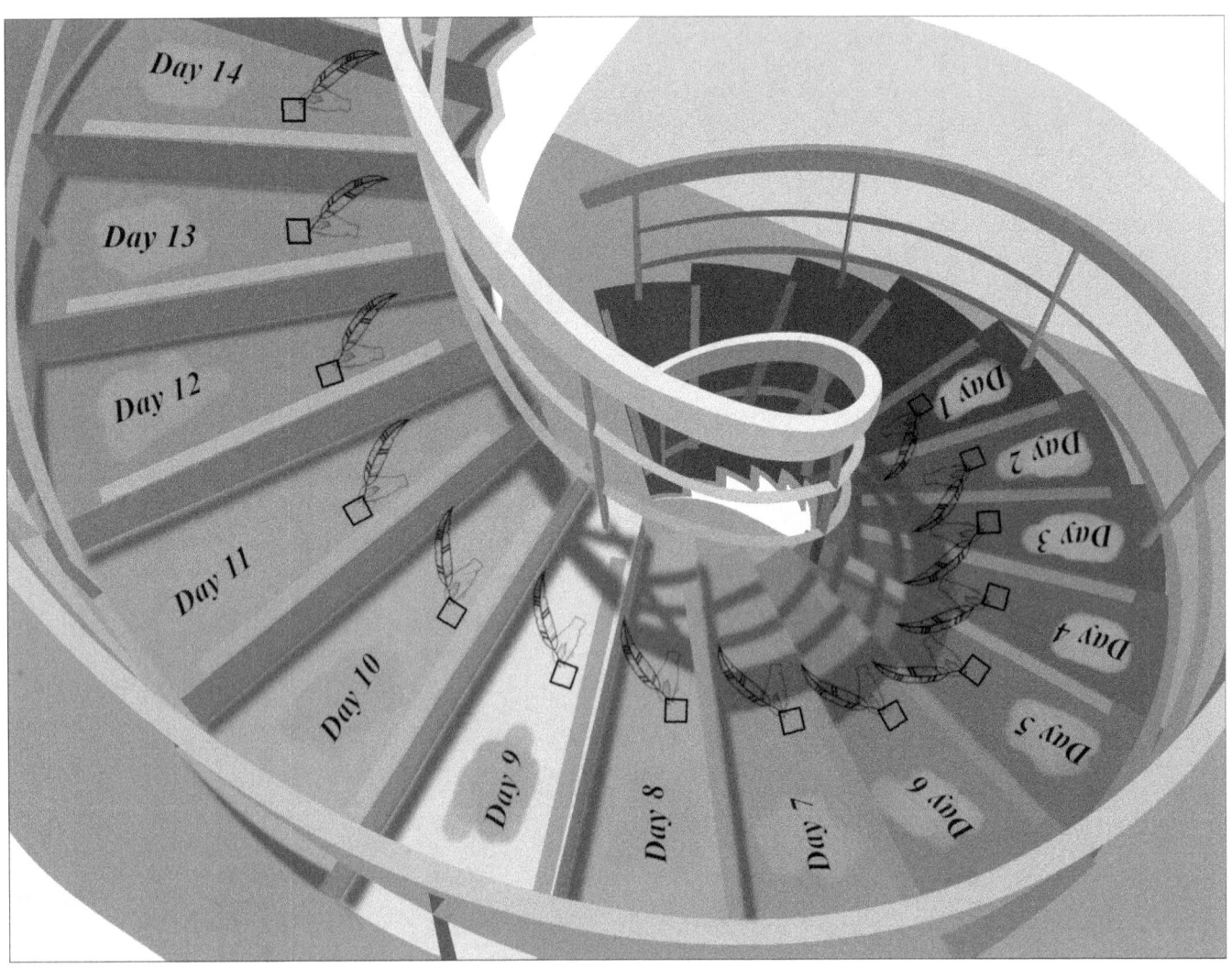

Lesson 16: Faithfulness, Consistency, and Dependability

Quotes

"A woman's function is laborious, but because it is gigantic, not because it is minute I will pity Mrs. Jones for the hugeness of her task; I will never pity her for its smallness." –G.K. Chesterton (from an essay entitled "The Emancipation of Domesticity")

"One cannot always be a hero, but one can always be a man." –Johann Wolfgang von Goethe[lvi]

"The greatest thing a man can possibly do in this world is to make the most possible out of the stuff that has been given him. This is success, and there is no other. It is not a question of what someone else can do or become which every youth should ask himself, but what can I do? How can I develop myself into the grandest possible manhood?" –Orison Swett Marden, 1911 essay "Wanted—A Man"[lvii]

"Every right implies a responsibility; every opportunity, an obligation; every possession, a duty." –John D. Rockefeller[lviii]

"The hand that rocks the cradle is the hand that rules the world." –William Ross Wallace

Lesson 17

The Eighth Commandment of Chivalry: You shall be honest and keep your word

Bible Reading

Ephesians 4:25
Proverbs 11:3
Proverbs 28:13

"It...it was I who let the goat in," Guibert almost **choked** on the words and felt his hands shaking with fear as he spoke to his uncle. He could feel the astonished stares of the crowd. To Guibert, telling the truth at that moment took much more courage than fighting Étienne and the wolves had. "His name is Ratramnus... Er...Sir Ratramnus?"

The sound of sniggering came from somewhere in the crowded hall. Sir Enguerrand turned a strange shade of red and even raised his hand to hit Guibert before he stopped himself and brought it down. "You will have scullery duty, boy. Father Thomas, can knighting a goat be undone?"

"I...er...I...um... Oh, dear! I don't really know, my lord... I don't think anyone has ever knighted a goat before," the priest replied in confusion.

More people in the crowd laughed, and one **bold** fellow even shouted out, "Shouldn't you buckle on his belt and sword now, milord!"

"'Tis no laughing matter. Someone escort this thing..."

"Maaaaaa!"

"Seize yon knighted goat!" yelled out someone.

"Meeeh!"

"...get that goat back to its pen!" thundered the knight.

"Mwaaaaaaa!"

"You, Guibert of Ghent, come with me."

Sir Enguerrand led Guibert to the solar where they could be away from the **crowds** and demanded an explanation. Guibert told him the whole story and said he was very sorry.

"You were brave to tell the truth, Guibert, but... Do you realize Chrétien is the favorite nephew of my worst enemy, Sir Achard Talcott?"

Lesson 17: The Eighth Commandment of Chivalry

Guibert did not. That was **bad**.

"Chrétien is probably riding off in fury to tell Achard how I humiliated him on the day of his knighting."

That was **really bad.**

"And because that old fiend will welcome any excuse for a fight, he'll probably gather an army of knights to attack us as soon as he can."

> Draw a man peeking out of a secret passage.

That was **really, *really* bad.**

"And if that were not enough to fret over, half the castle now knows about the secret passage under a flagstone behind my chair in the hall! And the other half will know soon enough. That passage was made for the castle's defense by my grandsires. Generations have guarded the secret that it exists. It opens into the woods so the family can escape in time of siege. But now I shall have to wall it off, so no one can come into the keep from outside!"

Sir Enguerrand finished by saying he might have to send Guibert back home if he couldn't do his duties faithfully. But he was a kind man at heart and understood the goat incident had been an accident. For now, Guibert would only have to do kitchen work for two more weeks as punishment.

That night Guibert lay awake upon his bed of rushes in the great hall, staring at the moonlight through a high, barred window above him and thinking of the trouble he'd gotten into. He couldn't sleep. Part of the reason was Zwane's croaky **snoring** in his pocket. He was probably dreaming about tasty flies and juicy earthworms. But the scurrying sounds of rats and creatures of the night in the stairways and corners of the hall…and the walls…did not help the boy sleep either. The walls… Were those rats in the walls? Guibert thought about the secret passage. BUMP! That sounded so loud it had to come either from a rat the size of a donkey or…something else.

Guibert stood up and pressed his ear to the wall. He thought he heard a muffled voice and the small tinking sound of a **hammer** on stone. His skin crawled and the hairs on his arm stood up.

"Gadsbudlikins! Is the castle **haunted** like Dame Blanche always says?" he whispered.

There was a soft creaking sound on the other end of the dais. A light, ever so faint, came from a crack in the stone floor behind Sir Enguerrand's chair. The other pages and servants snoring in the hall did not stir. Guibert squinted and **slid** forward to peek around Sir Enguerrand's chair for a better view. There was a flicker, as of candlelight coming from beneath the floor. Then he realized quite suddenly that there were also two **eyes** staring at him from underneath the raised flagstone. They met his gaze briefly then disappeared. The stone dropped with a slight "CLACK!" Guibert gasped aloud.

The terrified page boy ran out of the hallway, up a spiral staircase, and toward the solar where Sir Enguerrand and Lady Ermingard slept. He pounded the oaken door furiously and was answered by an angry servant, who boxed him immediately in the ear.

"'Ere now, fonkin boy! Wha' mean ye a-wakin' the lord and lady at this hour?"

"We…we are beset by enemies…or ghosts maybe. *Someone* is in the secret passage in the hall! Please, please tell Sir Enguerrand!"

Sir Enguerrand himself was at the door by this time, wrapping a cloak about him and glaring in the **darkness** at Guibert. But when he heard the boy's story he hurried to get dressed and ordered torches lit.

"Normally I'd have a page boy soundly thrashed and put back to bed…" the knight muttered to his wife as he buckled on his sword. "But earlier today this lad told me the **truth** even though he knew it would harm him. There may be something amiss!"

It seemed an age before the knight was dressed and he and Guibert made their way to the great hall. Enguerrand had already sent the servant for Rollo the steward, and they came only half a minute behind them. The slumbering servants and page boys were roused and told to light torches and candles. Sir Enguerrand, meanwhile, crossed directly to the dais, Guibert scurrying along behind him trying to keep up. He raised his **torch** to stare at the stone floor. Everything looked in place. He bent down and pushed aside the false panel in the floor that hid an iron ring. He lifted the ring and the largest flagstone in the floor opened with it, showing a black hole open into the recesses of the castle floor. It was silent as the **grave**, with the hint of a chill draft exhaling from it, but no hint of light or movement.

Sir Enguerrand ordered the servants to check the castle for anything amiss. He motioned to Rollo, then glanced at Guibert. "Come, boy." He drew his sword and dropped down into the darkness. Guibert climbed after him, finding a short iron ladder built into the stone wall, and the steward dropped down after him.

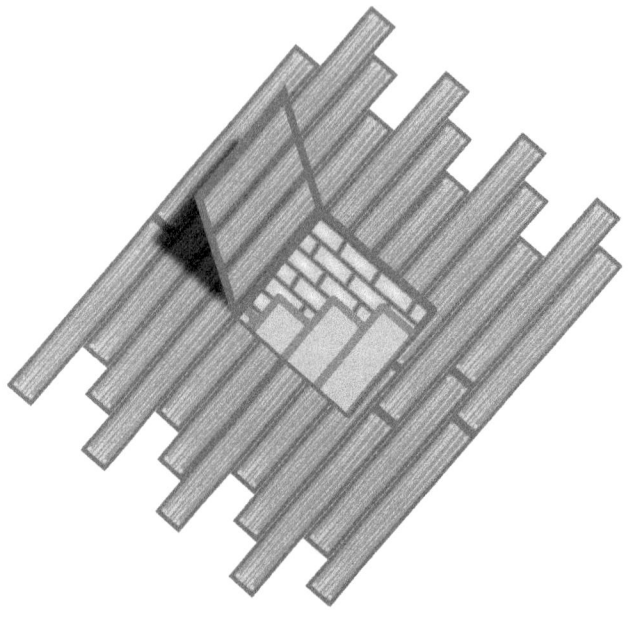

Lesson 17: The Eighth Commandment of Chivalry

Think about it, talk about it

Do you think it was hard for Guibert to tell the truth? Did telling the truth keep him from getting into trouble?
_____
_____
_____

How did telling the truth end up helping Guibert? *
_____
_____
_____

Do you think Guibert really saw someone in the secret passage at Château Bon-heur? What do you think someone might be doing in the secret passage?
_____
_____
_____

Dust off your quill crayon

Chess is a very old game. Do you know how to play it? Noble people in the Middle Ages loved to play chess. Sometimes they even gambled over chess games! Color this picture of a lord and lady playing chess!

Lesson 17: The Eighth Commandment of Chivalry

Quest of the Day

Find the hidden words.

A	H	I	A	L	K	R	H	E	L	N	E	K	E	C	K	S	E
E	C	A	S	T	L	E	K	O	K	R	N	T	N	W	A	L	I
D	S	F	N	X	P	W	N	E	N	G	S	L	T	N	L	N	Y
D	S	G	H	T	J	N	Z	N	H	O	N	E	S	T	Y	T	I
A	N	D	W	C	X	T	Y	U	Y	A	R	D	B	C	I	I	N
F	X	O	V	Y	S	T	D	G	U	T	J	I	B	V	N	C	G
F	K	N	I	G	H	T	D	U	X	C	P	J	D	F	G	E	V
A	U	Y	W	N	E	N	N	C	L	E	M	V	D	N	O	L	L

CASTLE HONOR
GOAT   KNIGHT
HONEST LYING

Memory Verse

"You shall not bear false witness against your neighbor." –Exodus 20:16

Quotes

"Honesty is the first chapter in the book of wisdom." –Thomas Jefferson[lix]

"Honesty is more than not lying. It is truth telling, truth speaking, truth living, and truth loving." –James E. Faust[lx]

"Every man of courage is a man of his word." –Pierre Corneille[lxi]

"If the youth should start out with the fixed determination that every statement he makes shall be the exact truth; that every promise he makes shall be redeemed to the letter; that every appointment shall be kept with the strictest faithfulness and with full regard for other men's time; if he should hold his reputation as a priceless treasure, feel that the eyes of the world are upon him, that he must not deviate a hair's breadth from the truth and right; if he should take such a stand at the outset, he would…come to have almost unlimited credit and the confidence of everybody who knows him." –Orison Swett Marden, 1911 essay "Wanted—A Man"[lxii]

Lesson 18
Honesty

Bible Reading
Luke 16:10-12
Proverbs 12:17-19

Lying is telling people things that are not true, things you know do not match with reality. The Eighth Commandment of Chivalry teaches us to never lie and to be people known for telling the truth. "You shall be honest and keep your word."

Being Trustworthy

A chivalrous person will be someone who is trustworthy—a grown-up word that means somebody who always tells the **truth**. You can trust that person to tell the truth. Being trustworthy is a path to honor. We often use the grown-up word "honorable" to mean trustworthiness. An honorable person with a good reputation is a person known for keeping their word.

Draw a sneaky snake.

There is nothing that can break a good reputation like being known as a **liar**. If you lie enough times people will stop believing you, like "the boy who cried wolf." Every lie will move you closer to being known as a person who cannot be trusted: a person without honor.

People of Our Word

A chivalrous man keeps his **promises**. This is what it means to be "a man of your word." A chivalrous man takes his words very seriously. If he says he will do something, he will do it. He will when it's easy and when it's hard. You only become a "man of your word" by keeping your promises when keeping them is difficult. Anyone can keep their word when **it costs** them nothing. But you prove yourself trustworthy when you keep your word though it is embarrassing or harmful to you. Guibert of Ghent did this when he told the truth about Ratramnus, even though it caused him to be punished. And Sir Enguerrand understood that to be a sign that Guibert was trustworthy, and later believed his story about an intruder in the secret passage when he otherwise might not have.

Being serious about our promises means we must be **careful** about what we say. The Bible tells us our words are very powerful, and that controlling our tongue is one of the best ways we show the virtue of self-control.

"For we all stumble in many ways. And if anyone does not stumble in what he says, he is a perfect man, able also to bridle his whole body. If we put bits into the mouths of horses so that they obey us, we guide their whole bodies as well. Look at the ships also: though they are so large and are driven by strong winds, they are guided by a very small rudder wherever the will of the pilot directs. So also the tongue is a small member, yet it boasts of great things. How great a forest is set ablaze by such a small fire!" (James 3:2-5).

Our words can **hurt** people blacks or they can **build** people up. They can get us into all kinds of trouble, or they can give us a reputation of wisdom and honor. Because of the power of our words, it's smart to be careful what we say. Try to get into the habit of **thinking** about what you say before you say it. Keep words back that you want to say if they are not completely true or helpful. It is often better to say nothing than to say something untrue or hurtful. James 1:19 cautions, "Know this, my beloved brothers: let every person be quick to hear, slow to speak, slow to anger."

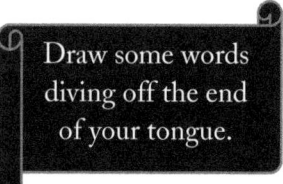

A chivalrous person is sincere, that is, he means what he says. He does not play games with people and tell them things he doesn't mean. He does not joke around by lying, and then say he was just kidding. He does not use his words in sneaky ways that bend the truth to get things he wants.

God is Truth

The most important reason to keep the Eighth Commandment of Chivalry is that God only speaks truth (John 16:13). He loves truthfulness: His very **nature** is true. We ought to love the truth as we ought to love God. And when we mold our characters into truthfulness and become people of our word, we become more than honorable: we become like our Father in heaven.

Habits of Honor

Are you a person of your word? Start today to develop habits of honesty:

- If your dad says no to something, don't ask your mom the same thing hoping she won't know. This is dishonest.
- Don't say things that are partly true, but not quite true. A half-truth is a whole lie!
- Listen more.
- Stop and think before you say something, especially before you promise something.

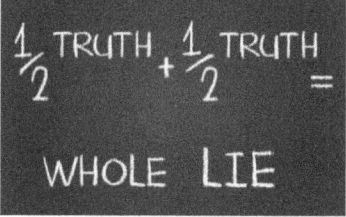

- Avoid making big promises or swearing to do something. Try to speak simply and mean it.
- Avoid the trap of "just kidding": most of the time saying something and taking it back is a poor joke that just confuses others and makes you look a dishonest fool.
- Keep track of your promises, and do them as soon as possible (so you don't forget).

Think about it, talk about it

Read John 8:44. What nickname does Jesus give the devil in this verse? Why do you think the devil is called that? *

_____
_____
_____

Do you remember a time someone told you something that wasn't true? Do you remember how you felt? Do you think others feel bad if you tell them a lie?

_____
_____
_____

What should you do if you have already told a lie?

_____
_____
_____

Lesson 18: Trustworthiness

Dust off your quill crayon

Color these medieval gals!

Dust off your quill crayon part 2

Now color these medieval dudes!

Lesson 18: Trustworthiness

Quest of the Day

Can you think of 3 people who are famous in history for being truthful, trustworthy, and honorable? (Some people I thought of are in the answers at the back of the book.) Write their names in this frame, and draw a picture of one of them.

Quotes

"There is nothing so strong or safe in an emergency of life as the simple truth." –Charles Dickens[lxiii]

"Be silly. Be honest. Be kind." –Ralph Waldo Emerson[lxiv]

"Honesty, truth and decency all link together- by loving all of these, we can improve our families, communities and our society." –Estella Eliot, *Positively Christian*[lxv]

"No legacy is so rich as honesty." –William Shakespeare[lxvi]

From *The Boy's King Arthur* by N.C. Wyeth.

Lesson 19

The Ninth Commandment of Chivalry: You shall be generous, and give largesse to everyone.

Bible Reading

Deuteronomy 15:10
2 Corinthians 9:8

A rat scurried out of the shadows and made Guibert jump. **Cobwebs** clung to him as they passed around dark corners, and he could hear the steady dripping of water from somewhere. Guibert almost regretted following Sir Enguerrand into the secret passage. It was a **spooky** place, with damp air and strange echoes. The flickering torchlight even lit upon the grinning skull of a poor dog who had gotten into the walls ages ago and never found his way out.

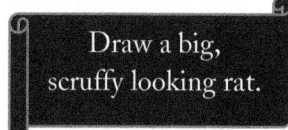

Draw a big, scruffy looking rat.

"Ribbit!" Zwane commented from the recesses of Guibert's pocket as if to say, "Nice digs! A chap could be comfortable here, in good sooth!" And it was just the sort of clammy, dark place a toad would like.

They twisted and turned through narrow ways not much wider than Guibert's shoulders for what seemed a long time.

"Ho there! Is someone here?" Sir Enguerrand called out suddenly. No answer came but the scuffling echoes of hurried **footsteps**. It was unnerving to think they were running through the very walls Guibert walked past every day, and never knew there was a secret behind them. He wondered how many people had used this hidden passageway in the castle's long history. They came to a narrow stairway that led down into deeper darkness and followed it.

The stone steps ended in a long, dark corridor. A sudden flash of dawn concentrated at the far end of the corridor. A face appeared just as suddenly. Someone had opened a hatchway at the secret tunnel's exit. Guibert caught his breath as he recognized the face. It was Chrétien.

The former squire narrowed his eyes into a scowl and pointed at Guibert. "I remember you, boy! You've troubled me for the last time!" he hissed, before leaping up into the light.

A sudden snapping sound was followed by darkness. They knew he had closed the trap door. The knight and steward ran to catch up with the fiend. There was a scraping sound and a loud **thump** above them, and they found the trapdoor wedged firmly shut. They set their shoulders against it but it would not budge.

"The villain has knocked a boulder or something against the door!"

There was nothing for it but to go back the way they'd come. They wound their way back through the dank, narrow ways toward the Great Hall.

"Zooterkins!" exclaimed Rollo as they scuffled along in the torchlight. "What was yer squire a-doin', sir?"

"I can scarce guess," the knight replied. "Have you any idea, Guibert? He threatened you."

"Aye. I think he's still mad at me for when I stopped him from bullying young Odo's friend, my lord, and for **messing** up his knighting ceremony. But I have no idea why he was in here… I have heard Dame Blanche complain of strange noises in the walls. Mayhap he has been in here before?"

Sir Enguerrand stopped and scratched his chin in thought. "Impossible. Until that **crazy goat** came up through the entrance in front of all my household, I and my lady were the only ones who knew about this passageway. It was a closely guarded family secret."

It was Guibert's turn to think, and he fell silent as they slid along the chilly stone of the passageway. A thought popped into his mind as he thought about what his uncle had said earlier about Chrétien.

"Sir Enguerrand… Didn't you say Chrétien was Sir Talcott's nephew?"

"I did."

"Do you think Chrétien was here to spy for Sir Talcott, like Étienne?"

"I suppose 'tis possible…"

They were inside Château Bon-heur's walls again and could hear the faint **echo** of people moving around on the other side. It was funny to think they probably had no idea there were three people behind the wall. There was also the sound of running water… Hadn't Ratramnus come in here from the drain? Guibert moved to where the water sounded loudest and bent down to feel the wall with his fingers. A damp opening met him in the shadows.

"I think animals have been coming in the passageway through here," he said.

The steward bent his torch down to reveal a gap in the stone about the height of Guibert's waist. "Faith! Look 'ere!"

"An opening has worn out by the **runoff** from the drains," Sir Enguerrand commented. "Years of water weathering the rocks at this bend must have opened it up." He ran a finger over the edge of the gap and it came up covered in a white powder. "Flour!"

"Then Ratramnus did come through here!" Guibert exclaimed, looking through the hole curiously.

"All very interesting," said Rollo. "But what I want to know is why that squire came in here."

Guibert took a deep **breath** to gulp down his fear, then stuck his head into the hole. He thought he saw a yellow gleam in the torchlight on the other side of the hole. His mouth fell open with a sudden, strange thought.

Lesson 19: The Ninth Commandment of Chivalry

"Uncle…Would Sir Talcott perchance have any claim to Château Bon-heur if he married Asceline?"

"Well, she would inherit the castle next to my son Odo. What do you mean by this, lad?"

"Maybe Dame Blanche *has* been hearing someone knocking on the walls at night…" Guibert mused, not exactly answering the question.

Guibert asked Rollo to hold the torch closer. He **leaned** further into the hole. He could see something glittering far away into the darkness.

"Why on earth would someone go about knocking on walls at night?" Rollo asked.

> Draw a secret underground chamber.

"I think I know…" Guibert felt excited. He had to hold his breath to **wiggle** his torso through the little hole. His voice came echoing out into the secret passage when his waist was through. "You once told me the story of Asgeir the Viking, who looted many churches and villages in these parts. And no man knew for sure what became of his riches." Guibert squeezed the rest of his body through the little opening and reached back through it for the torch.

Cold water trickled down on his head, and he could feel an opening downward at his heels. He was standing on a ledge before a deep hole of some kind.

He raised the torch. A small hidden **chamber** opened before him, built above the secret passage. A stone arch held up the ceiling some four feet above his head, and a square drain in this side of the ceiling directed a small waterfall into a bowl-shaped drain on the chamber's floor near him. Guibert raised the torch higher, and looked across to the other side of the chamber… And gasped aloud.

"Guibert! What are you doing, lad? Are you alright?" Sir Enguerrand and Rollo called in alarm.

Guibert put his head out into the passage again. "'Tis wondrous, Sir Enguerrand! A hidden chamber…"

"A hidden chamber in a secret passage?" Rollo whispered, amazed to find such double mysteries hidden within the castle he'd spent so many years managing.

"A treasure chamber!" Guibert exclaimed, and held his hand out. It was full of glimmering jewels, ancient gold coins, and a **crucifix** of gold.

Both grown men clambered to peek into the little hole Guibert had climbed in. Then they saw it too, tucked in a little nook carved upon the side of the chamber… A massive chest, ancient and rotted, lay upon the other side of the little room, and it was piled high with gleaming riches.

"Gold coins, bars of silver, a crown of some sort, gilded crosses, jewels of many colors, pearl necklaces, a Viking sword…" Guibert recited as he ran his small hands through the chest and fumbled through its riches in numb amazement.

"The horde of Asgeir!" Sir Enguerrand whispered. "Walled up inside Château Bon-heur all these years!"

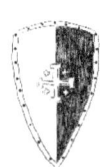

Sir Enguerrand managed to keep the treasure secret for a few days, which was enough time for the steward and two trusted **servants** to break down the wall to the hidden chamber and carry all the treasure to the knight's counting-house where it was put under lock and key. Word got about quickly of the hidden Viking horde, though, and the countryside was soon buzzing with the news. Everyone wondered what Sir Enguerrand was going to do with the newfound wealth.

Draw a Viking treasure in your secret chamber.

Guibert was called to his uncle's chamber a couple of days after the find and was amazed to be handed a leather purse of gold **coins** and an ancient jeweled **dagger**. It was more wealth than Guibert ever dreamed of owning.

"We'd never have found the treasure had it not been for you, lad. You deserve a share," Sir Enguerrand told him.

"Th…thank you!" Guibert stammered.

"And I want you to take this purse of coins to that gatward friend of yours. Will you do that, lad?"

Indeed he would! The boy was amazed at such **generosity** and knew it would change Humbert and his poor family's lot for a long time.

"I've turned half of the treasure over to my almoner," the knight continued. "He will use it to improve the lot of the poor families on my manor.[24] Among his many useful plans for the gold, he will build a mill for the poor, and a public garden and **fishery** so they will have more food every year. I thought you'd like to know that." He put a hand on the boy's shoulder, which Guibert knew by this time was his uncle's signal for a knightly lecture. "You see, young Guibert, chivalry demands a knight be open-handed. He must be generous to all around him and not horde wealth for himself."

Guibert was glad to see such noble **kindness** in his uncle and vowed in his heart to become generous like him. He went straight away and gave the gatward family the bag of coins from Sir Enguerrand. Both Humbert's father and mother wept aloud at how this would improve their family. Guibert left their hovel with a happier heart, glad to help and serve others. He was glad also at the thought of all the good things to come for the poor folk living around Château Bon-heur.

That is, he was glad until he came nearer the keep and was hailed by a skinny man in brown robes who was standing next to an **oxcart** on which a rough cloth had been strewn over something hard and boxy. Two

---

[24] An almoner was a servant of a rich knight or lord whose job was to give alms (gifts of money and help and food) to poor people. He was a medieval social worker. The chaplain (priest of a castle) was usually the almoner's boss.

Lesson 19: The Ninth Commandment of Chivalry

soldiers with pikes stood nearby. He was wringing his hands and looked nervous. "Come here, page boy! I've an urgent job for you. I am Luke, Château Bon-heur's almoner, and I'm to make my way with these guards to Jumièges Abbey with Sir Enguerrand's treasure. It will be safer among the strong abbey walls and can be sold for the goods and the services I need to improve this manor. But I must send for Sir Enguerrand. I've just had news the **glint** of armor was sighted in the forest, not a league from here, and Midge the Forrester tells me that he saw Sir Talcott on road with an army. He is coming to steal the gold!"

Think about it, talk about it

Can you follow the trail of clues Guibert put together in his head to conclude that there was a Viking treasure hidden in the walls of the castle's secret passage? Some of them were early in this book. *

Was it wise of Sir Enguerrand to give half the Viking treasure to help the poor on his land?

Was it kind of Sir Enguerrand to give half the Viking treasure to help the poor on his land?

Was it noble of Sir Enguerrand to give half the Viking treasure to help the poor on his land?

What would you do with Viking treasure?

Lesson 19: The Ninth Commandment of Chivalry

Dust off your quill crayon

Here is a drawing of Martin of Tours by Léo Schnug. Martin of Tours, usually called Saint Martin, is famous for an act of kindness to a beggar and was a favorite symbol of charity to many medieval people. Can you tell what he is doing for the poor cold, beggar in the picture? Trace this picture and color it.

A painting of St. Martin and the beggar, by Gustav Adolf Closs.

Lesson 19: The Ninth Commandment of Chivalry

Quest of the Day

Cut out these medieval coins to play with. Pretend you're a knight giving generously to the poor. You might have to talk one of your brothers or sisters into pretending to be "The Poor." (There are color versions of the coins you can download to print from my website.)

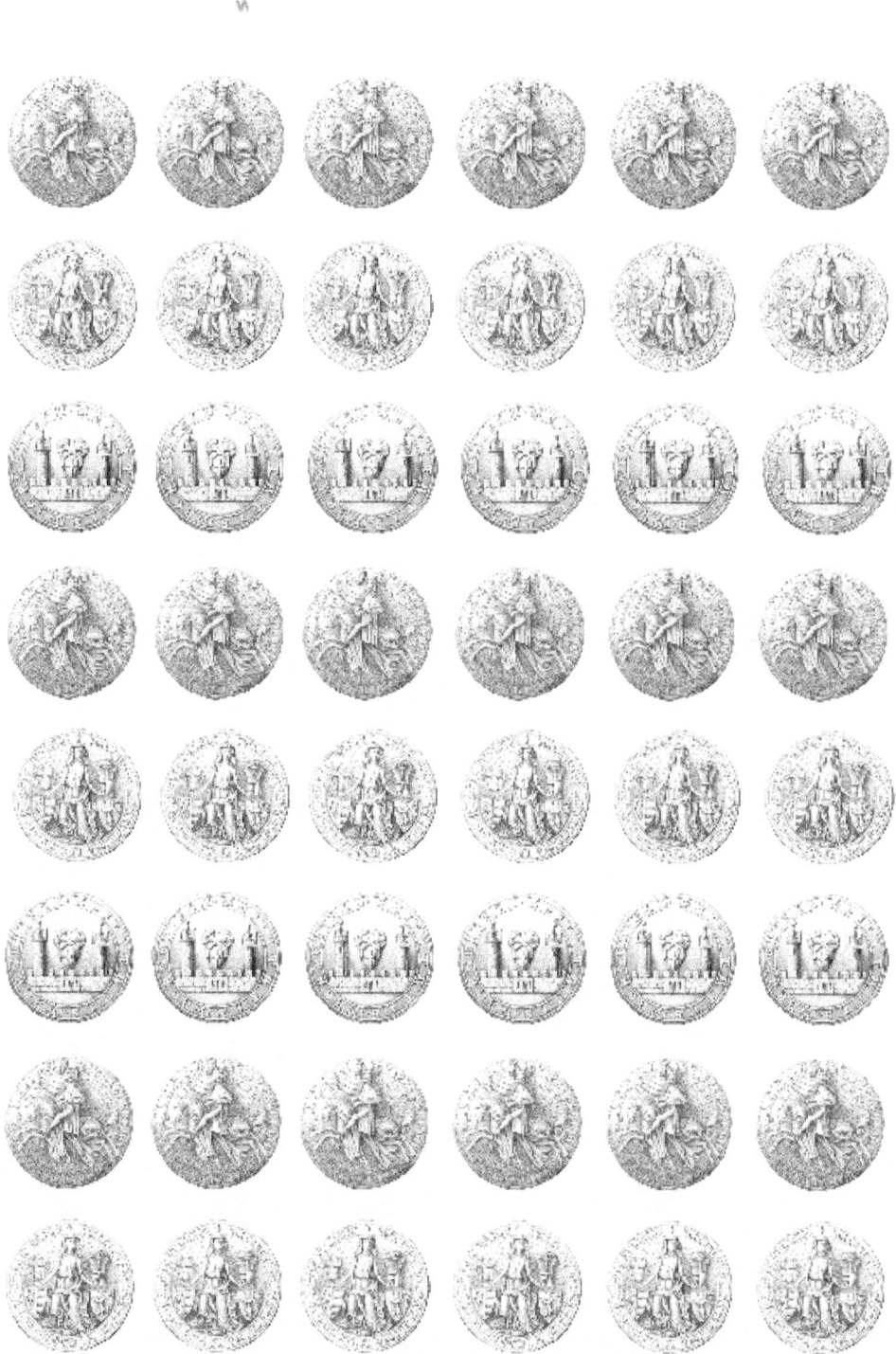

Memory Verse

"In the same way, let your light shine before others, so that they may see your good works and give glory to your Father who is in heaven." –Matthew 5:16

Quotes

"Then shareth he the wealth good store
That thence awayward he had brought,
And unto no man giveth nought,
That wealthy wax they, each, and hail."
–The anonymous *Ordene de Chevalerie*[lxvii]

"In fifty, in a hundred of our romances we find the same appeals, warm and impressive to all poor knights. 'Come, and you will be rich.' They came, and were enriched." –Leon Gautier

"However, the man to whom open-handedness and bravery both come naturally may indeed find himself momentarily in need but poverty will never harass him for long." –Geoffrey of Monmouth, 12th century[lxviii]

"Every day did she thus minister to the poor, bestowing a penny upon each, with a request that he would pray for the safety of her husband." –*Gesta Romanorum*, c. 13th century[lxix]

"He [Charlemagne] was very active in aiding the poor, and in that open generosity which the Greeks call alms; so much so, indeed, that he not only made a point of giving in his own country and his own kingdom, but when he discovered that there were Christians living in poverty in Syria, Egypt, and Africa, at Jerusalem, Alexandria, and Carthage, he had compassion on their wants, and used to send money over the seas to them." –Einhard, 9th century, from the *Vita Caroli Magni*[lxx]

Lesson 20

Largesse

Bible Reading
1 John 3:17

Hebrews 13:16

Proverbs 11:24

The Ninth Commandment of Chivalry tells us to "be generous, and give largesse to everyone." Do you know what **generosity** is? Generosity is just a big word for giving things to people, especially people in need. Do you know what largesse is? That's an older word that even grown-ups don't use much anymore (so if you learn it you will be smarter than many of them). It means giving *in a large way* to people in need. It is generosity with flare and **joyfulness**.

Draw a knight throwing coins to people at a wedding.

In the Middle Ages largesse was an important part of a noble person's life. They gave to the poor at weddings and knighting ceremonies and baptisms. They tithed to the church. They even kept permanent almoners to give regular gifts to the poor on their fiefs.

God Gives Largesse

God is the best example of chivalric largesse. He is generous to everyone, even to His enemies. He is an open-handed Heavenly father who gives His children good things, more than any father on earth can do (Matthew 7:9-12). When we give generously we become more than chivalrous: we start **looking like** our Heavenly Father.

Tithe

One particular type of largesse God commands us to give in the Bible is tithe. He tells us to give from our income back to him in the form of tithes at church. This is not a troublesome duty when we remember that everything we have comes in the first place is from God. Tithing is a way to show that we believe this. Tithing is also a great honor because it makes us part of the church's mission to further God's kingdom. It is an exciting and almost magical way of turning physical coins, the fruit of physical work, into **spiritual** good to others and spiritual reward.

"Whoever is generous to the poor lends to the LORD, and he will repay him for his deed" (Proverbs 19:17).

Charity and Smart Giving

Charity is more than somebody's name (though it is a nice name). It is a word for giving largesse to the poor and needy. God commands charity in the Bible in many different places and wants us to show a generous heart by the way we give to those we find in need. Largesse means more than just throwing some **coins** at a passing beggar. It is a way of thinking and an attitude of the heart that chivalry demands of us. We should be happy to give, feeling honored to help others whenever we can. That is what Scripture means when it says that God "loves a cheerful giver."

But God also wants us to give **wisely**. It is unwise to give away what we need, and ungodly to give away what those depending on us need. We should give out of our excess, which is our extra money. This means that, as you grow older and get a job and start making money, you will need to **give** your tithe to God's church and take care of yourself and your family's needs first: then what is leftover is what you should give as largesse or charity. And what the Ninth Commandment of Chivalry teaches is that one of the goals of your job or career should be to make enough money to give away to those in need. To do this well, you will need to be smart in how you spend and save your money. So don't think of things like saving and making a budget (which is a written down plan for your money) as boring, grown-up things only: they are exciting ways to put your life's work to good use in obedience to God and honor to chivalry.

[Draw a kid puzzling over a budget.]

You should also learn, even at this time in your life, how to tell if someone really does need your help. Sadly there are many sneaky people in the world, as well as many **needy** people. And many of those sneaky people will try to trick you into giving to them when they don't intend to use your gift for good purposes. Chivalric giving requires that we be responsible in trying to find the people or organizations who need our help and give largesse in ways that will do the most good. Though we should be careful never to be so worried about sneaky people that we stop giving. Largesse means we're happy to give and **open-handed**. We give, and the people who benefit have a responsibility then to use what we give in smart ways.

Try Lots of Giving

There are lots of ways to be generous! Giving is not just about money. We give largesse when we **share** the things we have (like toys or food). We give largesse when we gladly give our time or skills to people by serving them.

So start becoming a boy or girl of largesse today! Develop habits of generosity by **sharing** your toys with your friends and siblings. Be ready to **help** people with your time or skills. Try to start **giving** some of the money you make, or your allowance (or however you acquire wealth at this time in your life).

Lesson 20: Largesse

Think about it, talk about it

What are some smart ways to show charity in your life right now? Especially think of ways you can help without having money.

Who do you know that might have a need you can help with? Make a plan with your mom and dad and go help them this week!

Have you ever made a budget? Ask your mom and dad to help you learn how.

Dust off your quill crayon

Quest of the Day

Make up several bags of non-perishable food items and keep them in your car. Give them away *(only when your mom or dad are with you)* to needy people you meet. Some ideas of items to include in your bags are:

- Applesauce
- Beef jerky
- Cheese or peanut butter crackers
- Fruit cups
- Granola bars
- Pudding
- Water bottles

You could even go the extra mile and put in something encouraging to read (which could be a tract or Christian pamphlet) and a blanket or coat. Often it's better to give people items they need than it is to give them money. Use this exercise to get in the habit of carrying extra items you can give away if the time is right.

Bonus Quest!

Turn the page to behold and marvel at five splendid chivalry bookmarks! Cut them out, color them, laminate them if you want to, and fold them in the middle to fit around your book pages. (If you can, download them in full color from my website to print.) Give them to your family and friends to hone your skills of largesse!

THE FIRST COMMANDMENT OF CHIVALRY

"YOU SHALL BELIEVE AND OBEY THE BIBLE, AND SHALL DEVOTE YOURSELF TO CHRIST."

THE THIRD COMMANDMENT OF CHIVALRY

"YOU SHALL BE GENTLE TO THOSE WEAKER THAN YOU, AND BECOME THEIR SELFLESS DEFENDER WHEREVER YOU FIND THEM."

THE FIFTH COMMANDMENT OF CHIVALRY

"YOU SHALL NOT RECOIL BEFORE THE ENEMY."

THE SEVENTH COMMANDMENT OF CHIVALRY

"YOU SHALL FAITHFULLY PERFORM YOUR RESPONSIBILITIES, AND SHALL HONOR ALL YOUR COMMITMENTS."

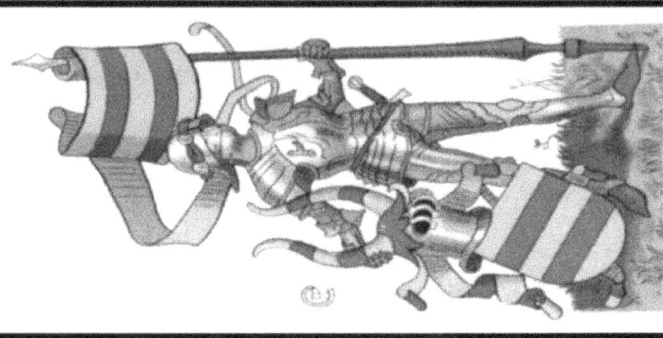

THE TENTH COMMANDMENT OF CHIVALRY

"YOU SHALL ALWAYS BE THE CHAMPION OF THE RIGHT AND THE GOOD, AND OPPOSE INJUSTICE AND EVIL WHENEVER AND WHEREVER YOU FIND IT."

Quotes

"That's what I consider true generosity: You give your all and yet you always feel as if it costs you nothing."
–Simone de Beauvoir[lxxi]

"You have not lived today until you have done something for someone who can never repay you."
–John Bunyan[lxxii]

"Do all the good you can,
By all the means you can,
In all the ways you can,
In all the places you can,
At all the times you can,
To all the people you can,
As long as ever you can."
–John Wesley, *Letters of John Wesley*[lxxiii]

"Money is but one venue for generosity. Kindness is an even more valuable currency." –Alan Cohen[lxxiv]

"There were two classes of charitable people; one, the people who did a little and made a great deal of noise; the other, the people who did a great deal and made no noise at all." –John Jarndyce, from *Bleak House* by Charles Dickens[lxxv]

Lesson 21

The Tenth Commandment of Chivalry: You shall always be the champion of the right and the good, and oppose injustice and evil whenever and wherever you find it

Bible Reading

Matthew 5:14-16

Proverbs 21:15

I hope you've never had to watch your **daddy** ride off into the woods to fight a powerful knight and his army. If you have, then I'm heartily sorry to hear it! It was a very scary thing for Asceline to see her daddy suit on his armor and mount upon his horse, ready to go risk his life with only Sir Jean (the newly-made knight), an old sergeant-at-arms named Andrew, ten spearmen, and a few peasants at his side. Sir Enguerrand left Rollo and five men-at-arms to defend the castle (the rest of his troop had been sent off on crusade). He would be greatly outnumbered by the villainous Sir Talcott, and the folk watching in the bailey were somber with the thought that their lord might not return from this mission alive. Guibert was going too. He sat on one of the fastest horses in Château Bon-heur's stables. A boy was needed to run messages back to the castle with news of the battle.

> Draw Sir Enguerrand on his horse, putting on his helmet.

Lady Ermingard **kissed** her lord and wept bitterly. "Must you go, Enguerrand? The risk is so great! Let Talcott take the treasure. We can wait out any assault he makes on the castle with you here."

"Nay, my good lady. We could not hold out for long against Talcott at the castle. He is a wealthy man and strong already, and ready to prosecute a siege. I'd not risk my family suffering at his hands. But if Midge is telling the truth, Sir Talcott is now in yon woods with only thirty men and thinks I don't know it. He is hoping to snatch away the treasure and begone without fuss. This is our chance to best him, and we won't likely find him so unprotected in the days to come. I must go. Talcott has shown his hand as our sworn **enemy**, and his villainy has gone far enough. I cannot stand by and let Talcott's unjust and wicked acts pass unchecked while breath

Lesson 21: The Tenth Commandment of Chivalry

is in me. What sort of knight would I be if I never risk life and limb in the cause of **justice**, sweet lady? Fare well, be safe!" He kissed her, then Asceline, then little Odo atop the head. He laced on his helmet and raised his arm with a warlike jingle (for it was covered in a glove and sleeve of chain mail), and signaled his band of soldiers to move out with the cart of treasure.

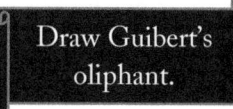

Guibert rode behind the knights and could hear Sir Enguerrand explain his battle plan to Sir Jean. Guibert wondered how he could be so calm and business-like.

"Sir Talcott has more soldiers than we do, but because he thinks nobody knows of his ambush we have the advantage of surprise. We must make good use of that advantage by ambushing his ambush."

"Er... I do not entirely follow."

"You will."

The plan became clearer when the bold knight ordered the treasure cart rolled out ahead of the soldiers, with only Luke the **almoner** and two soldiers with it. Sir Enguerrand and the rest of his men followed further behind, hidden in the trees.

It was a clear day, oddly pleasant for such deadly work. The leaves shimmered orange and brown and green overheard. The sun shone bright and warmed them against the cool of a slight breeze. Birds sang their fall songs. A badger scampered across the forest path. It was calm. But it was a deceptive calm. Guibert knew that the morning would end with **blood staining** the forest floor. He hoped the morning would end with justice done.

Inside himself, Guibert felt an interesting feeling. He felt angry but in a good way. He was angry at the bad deeds done by Sir Talcott: angry that a knight sworn to chivalry would try to steal Asceline, angry that he would plot against good men in Guibert's own country of Ghent, angry that he would try to steal gold meant to improve the lives of poor folk in order to enrich his already wealthy pockets. And because of those feelings, even though Guibert was scared about the pending fight, he was excited and proud to be part of it. He felt the thrill of having a **mission** worth sacrificing and fighting for.

It was not long before the fight came. A shout arose from the woodland road ahead of the knights, and they spurred their horses to a canter. Sir Enguerrand held up a hand to stop as they neared the sound of angry voices. They saw the treasure cart surrounded by mounted **warriors**. It was in a clearing in the woods where the road ran lower than the tree-line with a gentle ravine on either side. There were seven knights with swords drawn, and 15 footmen with axes and spears.

One of the knights sat upon a splendid white horse in a blue caparison (which is a special blanket covering a knight's horse). He was dressed splendidly, and held up a rich sword into the sunlight: and he was threatening Luke the almoner with it.

"That is Sir Talcott," Sir Enguerrand whispered, pointing to the man. "We need to cut him off from his troops and capture him quickly, and they all might surrender."

Two of the enemy knights dismounted and climbed up the wagon to look for the treasure.

"Can you blow an **oliphant**?"[25] Sir Enguerrand asked Guibert. Guibert said he could. "Stay hidden here. When you see us fighting among the enemy, I want you to blow your hardest upon this oliphant. They may mistake the call for reinforcements and panic." He put a hand on the lad's shoulder. "You are but a boy still, Guibert, you must stay out of the battle. If we lose and are killed or captured, ride straightway back to the castle to warn my family. Fare you well!"

Guibert nodded and took the horn **grimly**. Sir Enguerrand split the troop, he and Sir Jean taking up a point in the trees to the right of the wagon, and his footmen taking up a position to the left.

The two knights on the wagon lifted the blanket covering the treasure.

And then Sir Enguerrand and his troop attacked.

The knights burst forth from the trees, riding down to the road with a ferocious war cry ringing through the woodlands. The footmen came just after that, shouting as loudly as they could and leveling their spears as they charged. There was a brief moment when the enemy knights could only stare at the sudden foe in confusion. They had barely enough time to turn and pick up their weapons before the cunning warriors from Château Bon-heur were upon them.

There was a mighty **CLASH** of steel upon steel, which seemed to shake the very trees in the little clearing as the fight was joined. Spears were thrust into the surprised enemy, and men **screamed** aloud and fell wounded all around the cart with the first charge. The two soldiers guarding the wagon lifted their spears and thrust them right in the center of the enemy. The almoner pulled out an ax from beneath his robes to furiously whack at the villainous knights. Sir Jean and Sir Enguerrand came crashing into the group of knights with such force that Jean knocked down a rider with the sheer power of his horse ramming into him.

CRASH! SLASH! CRUNCH!

Sir Enguerrand let fly his sword all around him, with such speed and skill that it flashed in **rainbows of sparks** like Vulcan's hammer on either side of his saddle. Two of the knights fell wounded about him before he came to Sir Talcott and engaged him in a hand-to-hand duel.

"Ribbit! Rrriiibit!" Zwane the toad shouted as he peeked from Guibert's pocket. In his language, this almost surely meant, "Haha! Take that ye knaves! Have at ye, Poppinjays! Try my steel, ye fonkin-folk! Ha-HA!"

---

[25] An oliphant is a funny medieval name for a hunting horn.

Lesson 21: The Tenth Commandment of Chivalry

BAARROOOOOOOO! BAAAAROOOOOOO!!!!!!

Guibert set his lips to the oliphant and blew until he ran out of breath. That fearsome sound echoed from the dim woods so noisily it sounded like it came from all sides. And this was the final blow for most of Sir Talcott's henchmen. Every one of the foot soldiers still able to run turned and dashed away into the forest, certain an army of reinforcements would be hard upon their heels any moment. The knights in the wagon leaped down, forsook their chivalric courage and their liege-lord, and followed the foot soldiers in flight. Now there was only one knight fighting alongside Sir Talcott, and he was losing ground to Sir Jean's masterful sword strokes quickly.

CLASH! Jean's blade struck the enemy's sword so hard it nearly drove back into the foe's helm. SHING! With a deft turn of his wrist and a **shove** of the shield upon his left hand, Jean twisted the enemy's sword-blade around and trapped it between his sword and his shield edge. SHOOP! In nearly the same motion, he stabbed his sword forward and pierced his enemy's thigh. The brave enemy knight managed to keep his saddle and even ward off another blow from Jean until Luke the almoner suddenly jumped up and killed his horse with a ferocious blow to the poor beast's head. Horse and rider fell to the ground.

CRASH! Sir Talcott showed skill in spurring his horse to the side to avoid the fall of the knight beside him. CLING! He raised his **metal shield** edge and caught Sir Enguerrand's sword stroke above his head, before slashing out with a vicious strike of his own to Sir Enguerrand's waist. The strike missed by inches. SHING! Sir Enguerrand slid his sword off the edge of Sir Talcott's shield and swung it in an arch back around and under the shield. It was a good stroke, but it missed. However, Sir Enguerrand followed the stroke with a quick pull back of his hilt under the lip of his enemy's shield, jerking him forward in the saddle. Sir Talcott lost his balance and almost fell. He dropped his shield to the ground and lifted his sword for a counterstrike. Before he could strike, Sir Enguerrand spurred his horse in closer. With speed, he cast away his shield and brought the heavy **pommel** of his sword down hard upon Sir Talcott's head using both his hands.

There was a resounding RINNNNNG from the blow that bounced about the clearing. And as the reverberations of the blow died down, Sir Talcott gently slid from his saddle and fell heavily to the ground, knocked out cold by the force of Sir Enguerrand's blow.

For a moment all that could be heard were the sounds of the retreating foot soldiers (getting further and further away), and the moans of the wounded upon the ground. Then the warriors of Château Bon-heur let out a cheer that filled the woods. They had won the day!

"Take that wicked knight and tie him to his saddle," Sir Enguerrand ordered. "We will follow up this victory with another."

Chivalry: A Study for Little Knights

There were puzzled looks from Jean and the others, but they obeyed. Sir Enguerrand motioned for Guibert to come down and grinned at the boy as he entered the clearing. "Guibert, lad! Remember this day! Remember watching the cause of **right triumph** over wrong, and justice come upon the head of a wicked knight at last. You will someday use your sword and your strong arm to overcome wickedness and villainy with chivalric deeds. But our work is not over yet. King Henry has forces not far from here, and I mean to take Sir Talcott and turn him over to Henry's justice. He has been plotting with Henry's enemy, William Clito, and the king will be glad indeed to have him. You ride back to Château Bon-heur, Guibert, and tell Rollo and my family that I will be back with news upon the morrow."

And Guibert did just that. The castle **rejoiced** to hear news of Sir Talcott's downfall, but shut up the gates and kept careful watch that night for any attacks by the wicked knight's vassals.

1922 Illustration by N.C. Wyeth, from *The Boy's King Arthur*: the slaying of Sir Lamorak.

Think about it, talk about it

Do you think Guibert was right to feel angry at Sir Talcott's wicked deeds?

_____
_____
_____

Have you ever seen people fight with medieval longswords? Do you think a real fight between knights in the Middle Ages would be scary to watch?

_____
_____
_____

What does justice mean? *

_____
_____
_____

Dust off your quill crayon

This is a drawing by Morris Meredith Williams of the Battle of The Pass of Brander, in which the Scottish King Robert the Bruce fought against a Highland clan called the MacDougalls of Argyll. Color it!

Lesson 21: The Tenth Commandment of Chivalry

Quest of the Day

Have you ever wanted to learn to fight with a sword? Start now by learning a few basic longsword stances. Build a practice sword out of PVC and pipe padding, or just use a stick—but don't hurt anyone. Sir Enguerrand and Sir Jean used a one-handed sword with a shield in their battle in the woods. But the two-handed sword and the "hand-and-a-half sword" were becoming more and more popular in their day. The next two pages show some basic guard stances German swordsmen taught with the longsword.

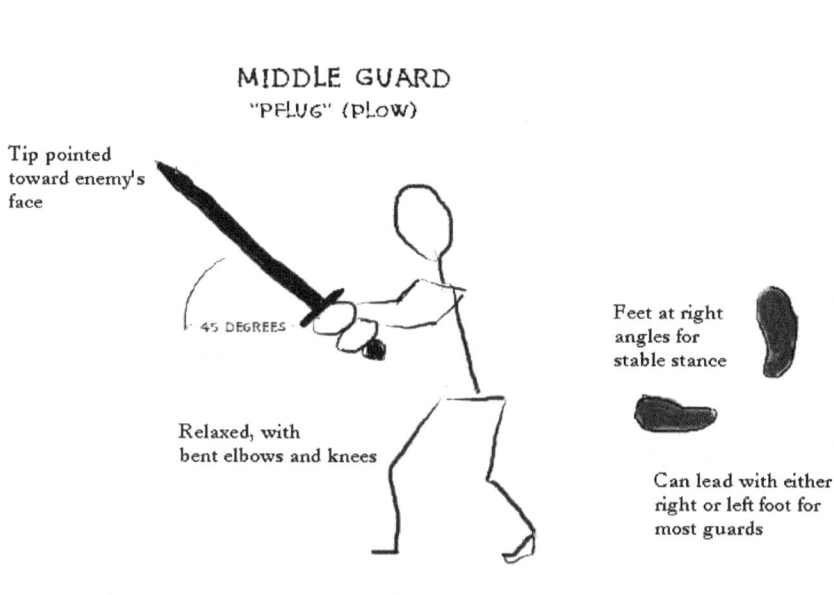

MIDDLE GUARD
"PFLUG" (PLOW)

Tip pointed toward enemy's face
45 DEGREES
Relaxed, with bent elbows and knees
Feet at right angles for stable stance
Can lead with either right or left foot for most guards

Blade out in front, facing opponent, foot forward. Most important and versatile guard, easy to transition to a range of parries and attacks.

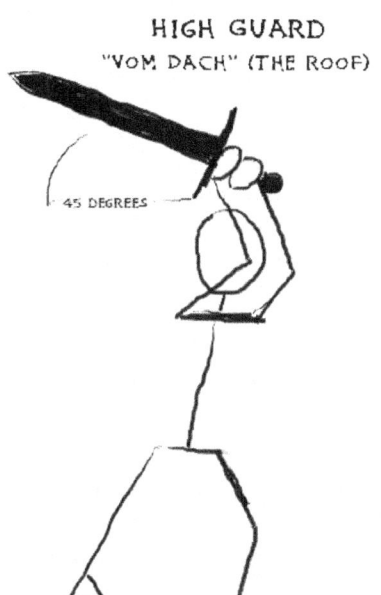

HIGH GUARD
"VOM DACH" (THE ROOF)

45 DEGREES

Pommel above forehead, blade above and behind you, menacing your foe and ready to strike down or circle out horizontally. A powerful and versatile position that can cut downward, horizontal, or low.

LOW GUARD
"EISERNE PFORTE" (IRON GATE)

Blade down and in front of you, leg forward, ready to strike upward or parry low. A useful guard for tempting opponent, guarding legs, thrusting or rising cuts, or simply resting

BACK GUARD
"SCHRANKHUT" (BARRIER GUARD)

Blade "hidden" behind you, edge outward, ready to strike or parry horizontally or upward. A difficult stance that is useful for tempting the opponent, while delivering strong upward or horizontal strikes

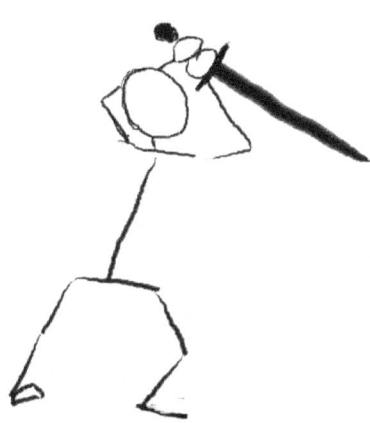

HANGING GUARD
"OCHS" (OX)

Pommel above your forehead, blade hanging point down in front of you, ready to parry in front, strike upward, circle around to strike or form new guard. Great for parrying attacks to the head, and delivering diagonal cuts

Memory Verse

"He has told you, O man, what is good; and what does the LORD require of you but to do justice, and to love kindness, and to walk humbly with your God?" –Micah 6:8

Quotes

"For noblesse of courage may not mount the high honor of chivalry without election of virtues and good habits." –Ramon Lull, *Knighthood & Chivalry*[lxxvi]

"As in the warfare of the Middle Ages, when each man was regarded as a power, so in the spiritual combats of all times, Chivalry requires every man to believe that he is personally called upon to pronounce between error and truth, injustice and justice, vice and virtue." –Kenelm Digby, *Maxims of Christian Chivalry*[lxxvii]

"To combat all evil, to defend all good' would not have come naturally to the minds of those descendants of Germans who had not been affected by the water of their baptism." –Léon Gautier

"O God, Thou hast only permitted the use of the sword to curb the malice of the wicked and to defend the right. Grant, therefore, that the new knight may never use his sword to injure, unjustly, anyone, whoever he may be; but that he may use it always in defence of all that is right!" –William Durand, in the 13th century *Benedictio novi militis,* ("Blessings of New Knights") quoted in *Chivalry*

From *The Boy's King Arthur* by N.C. Wyeth

Lesson 22
Your Quest

Bible Reading
1 Corinthians 10:31
Isaiah 1:17
1 Corinthians 3:16

"You shall always be the **champion** of the right and the good, and oppose injustice and evil whenever and wherever you find it." This Tenth Commandment of Chivalry is like a picture of all the rest of the commandments in one snapshot. It sums up the heart and the effect of all the others. We can, in fact, sum up the Tenth Commandment in one exciting word: "**quest**."

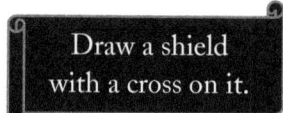

Draw a shield with a cross on it.

A quest is a mission. It is a goal glorious enough that you are ready to work hard to make it happen. Chivalry's main purpose is to inspire and direct us in the quest of *living for the glory of God and the good of other people*. All Ten Commandments of Chivalry are meant to lift our eyes from selfishness to selflessness: to work for things better than just seeking fun and stuff for ourselves. Chivalry helps us use our **earthly** efforts for **heavenly** good. Don't be afraid to take up that goal with all your heart. You really can't work too hard for it. There is no better quest than to love Jesus and to love other people because of Him. Remember that every effort you make toward that perfect quest is effort well spent.

Right and Wrong

More specifically the Tenth Commandment of Chivalry teaches a knight that he ought to know right from wrong and work in every way he can to help the right and hurt the wrong. This means he or she ought to be good, and follow God's law as perfectly as they can. A chivalrous knight should be "righteous"—a grown-up word that means he is known for living **God's ways**.

It's important to remember there is a real right and a real wrong. Many people will tell you differently. Some say that what you think is right is just made-up rules for you and aren't for other people. But this is not true. The rules God tells us in the Bible are true no matter what other people think of them. The Bible's rules and what it says is right is directly from the Creator of the universe, the one living true God. We are to live and promote his rules, not our own.

Draw a sword behind the shield.

Do you know what "justice" is? It's a word for bad acts getting punished and good acts getting rewarded in the proper ways. God Himself is the main dealer of justice. But He calls us (in verses like Micah 6:8) to live in ways that encourage justice: that help right things be rewarded and wrong things be discouraged. Justice will always result in the world becoming a better place than it was before.

It is important to remember that, in our excitement to help the **right and just** cause, we do not act unnecessarily nasty or unkind to people. We should always love other people and treat them courteously. But we should also care about God's ways. Part of our work is to teach other people His ways in a kind manner *because* **we care** about them.

> Draw a helmet hanging on the sword's handle.

The Battle Cry

So come along with me on this glorious adventure of chivalry! Lift your eyes beyond the here and now to the beautiful possibilities of what this sad world could look like **transformed** by God's goodness! Start now to train in every way you can find to bring that goodness about, and put away badness around you. Start in your own life, but don't stop by just making yourself a better person. Make the world around you better too! As we learn and follow God's ways we will become like Jesus. We will share more and more in His **thrilling mission** to fix this broken world and rescue people around us. And that is the exciting battle call of chivalry: come, little knight of today, and lift up your tired arms and give your strength and your skills to share in the good mission of your good Savior on earth!

From *The Boy's King Arthur* by N.C. Wyeth

Lesson 22: Your Quest

Think about it, talk about it

How will you learn what's right and what's wrong? *

Why is knowing what's right and wrong important to helping bring justice to the world? *

What about when you have been bad? Does making a mistake or doing something you know is wrong mean you can never be someone who promotes right and justice now?

Dust off your quill crayon

Quest of the Day

What are some ways you can promote justice and right in your life? Talk to your mom and dad. Write down and work for five specific "action items" that will promote righteousness and justice in your world. (Also available to print from my website.)

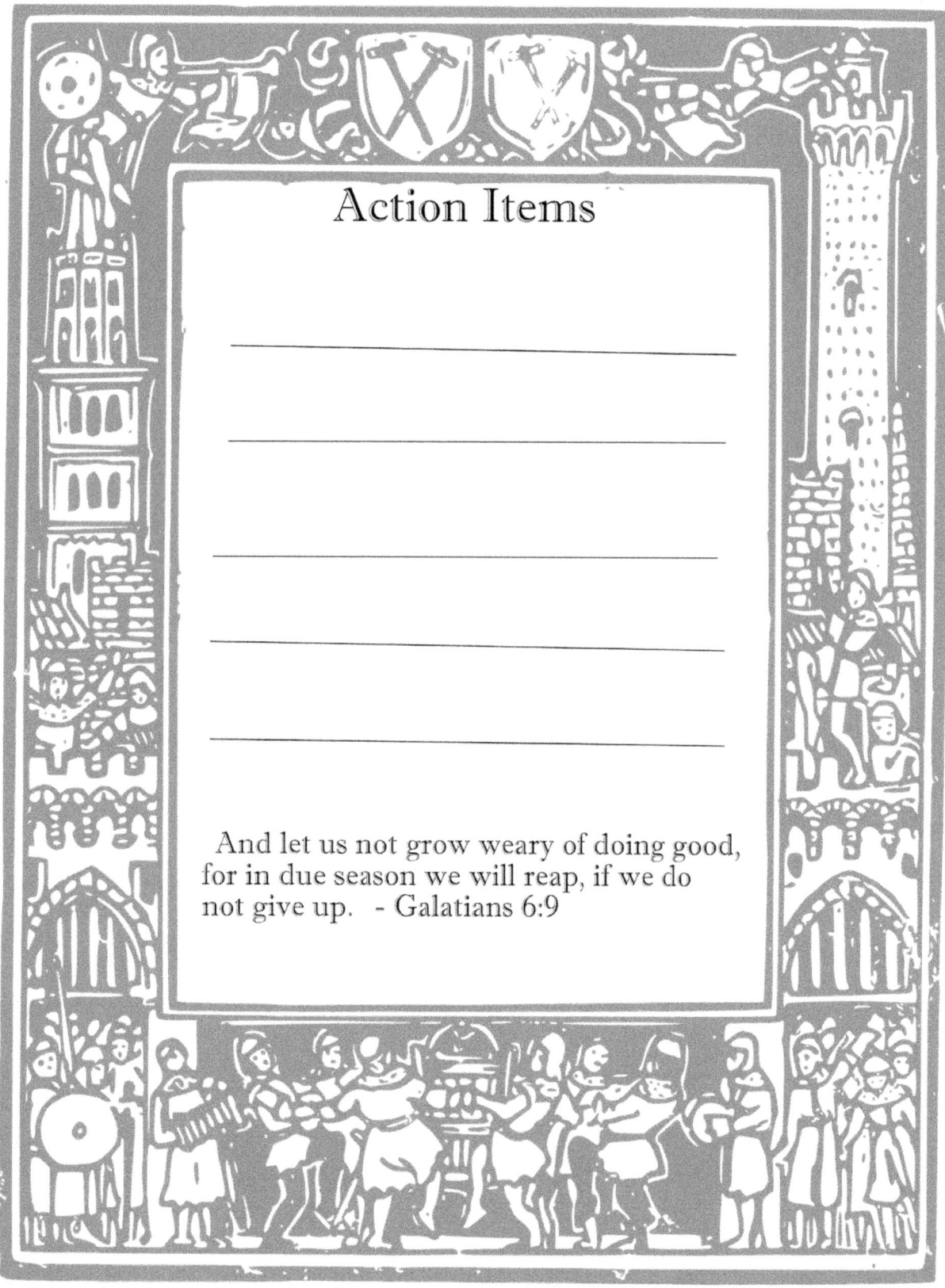

Action Items

And let us not grow weary of doing good, for in due season we will reap, if we do not give up. - Galatians 6:9

Quotes

"Lo, God! I am Thy handiwork. I have sinned and have done great evil, yet I am still Thy handiwork, who hath made me what I am. So, though I may not undo that which I have done, yet I may, with Thy aid, do better hereafter than I have done heretofore." –Howard Pyle[lxxviii]

"For every man may sin, and yet again may sin; yet still is he God's handiwork, and still God is near by His handiwork to aid him ever to a fresh endeavor to righteousness." –Howard Pyle[lxxix]

Epilogue

No attack came to Château Bon-heur during the night and day it took Sir Enguerrand and his troop to return to the castle. Sir Achard Talcott had been delivered to Henry I's justice and was taken to England as his prisoner. Months later he would be ransomed and returned to Rouen. But Henry I warned him if Talcott attacked Sir Enguerrand again he would have the Duke of Normandy and King of England to deal with (Henry I held both of these titles, you see). And this frightened Sir Talcott so very much that he was never a problem to Sir Enguerrand or his family again.

The treasure of Asgeir the Viking was delivered successfully to Jumièges Abbey and was put to very good use improving the lot of the poor upon Sir Enguerrand's land. This big act of generosity had the happy effect of raising the comfort of just about everyone on the manor and making it a more prosperous place for years to come.

Guibert of Ghent finished his seven-year training as a page and became a squire. He studied hard and served diligently, and eventually became a knight. He was a good knight, famous for his acts of chivalry. He did mighty deeds (in the wars against William Clito in Flanders especially). And he eventually won for himself a fief and castle of his own in his homeland of Flanders. It might be nice to say that Guibert married Asceline and had a passel of chubby Norman babies: but he didn't. Not every story ends that way. He did, however, marry another young lady named Beatrice, whom he loved very much, and they had four sons and three daughters.

Asceline married Sir Jean. She did eventually inherit Château Bon-heur, after the death of poor Odo when he was a teenager during a hunting accident. She and Jean's descendants ruled the castle and the fief around it well for generations and became famous as men and women of chivalry.

Oh, and Zwane ran away from Guibert the summer after the Viking treasure was found, and went on to become (so Sir Guibert later would tell his children) "a renowned and chivalrous knight in the court of Zwander, Toad-King of the Rouen's largest salt-marsh." He married a rich toad widow and had 47 tadpoles, all of which he taught the commandments of chivalry to, and one of which fought the dreaded newt lord of… But that's another story for another time…

Appendix A: Answer Key

Lesson 1

Why do you think knights would need a code to live by? They needed a code so they would have rules to teach them how God wanted them to use their strength in the right ways. This would help them know how to live and fight nobly.

Lesson 2

What is the difference between the history type of chivalry and the idea type of chivalry? History: rules used by knights in the Middle Ages. Ideal: the reasons behind the rules we can use in any age.

What are some ways the two definitions of chivalry are similar? Some examples: being a servant, helping others, obeying God's truth.

If chivalry is about using your strength, do you have to be strong to be chivalrous? Are there different ways to be strong? You do not have to be physically strong, but you do have to be strong in some ways. Some different ways to be strong: physically, mentally, will-power (not giving up), morally (resisting temptation), and emotionally (being strong despite circumstances).

How was the time in Israel that this verse was written about like the time in Europe after the Roman Empire fell? Everyone worshiped whatever gods they wanted, did evil things, and generally broke God's laws.

Answers to the crossword puzzle.

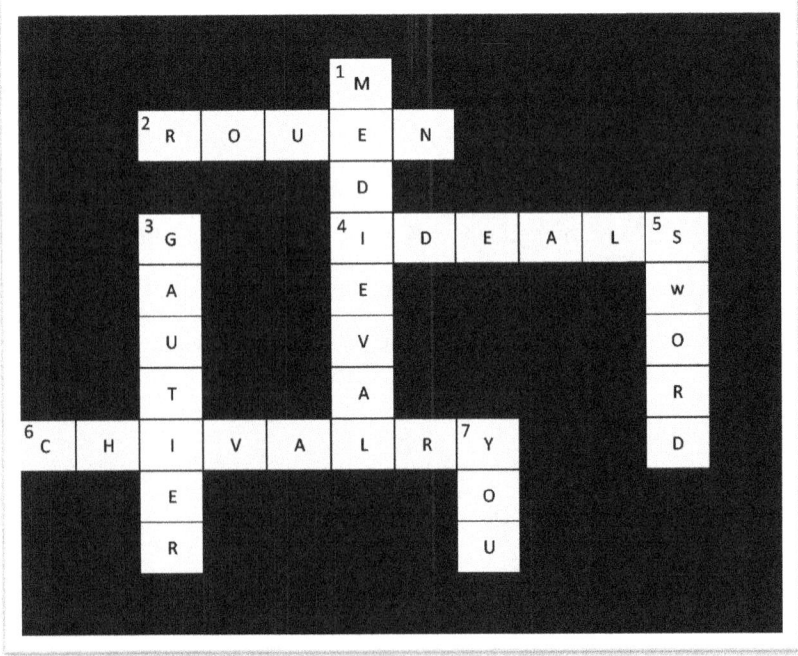

Lesson 3

What does it mean to fight with Jesus against the Devil? Some things this includes: working to stop bad things in the world and spreading the gospel (good news about Jesus). *What kind of fight is Jesus waging against the Devil?* A spiritual fight for people's souls.

What does it mean to say "chivalry is about doing?" Chivalry is about taking God's rules and putting them in action, going beyond just thinking/believing to actually living it in your life.

Answers to the quest of the day.

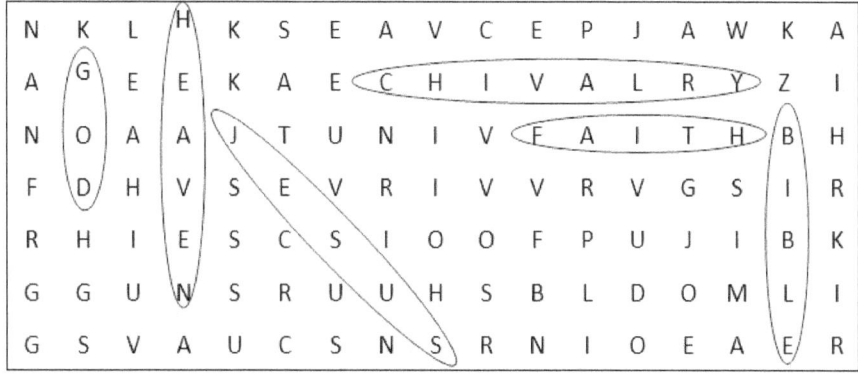

Lesson 4

Do you remember the definition of chivalry? "Codified Christian servanthood." *Why is it important to be Jesus' friend first, in order to learn chivalry?* Chivalry is first and foremost about following God.

What is God's Word? The Bible

Lesson 5

Were the Vikings always the bad guys? No! *Do you think they become Jesus' friends at some time?* Yes. It took a while, but eventually many of the Vikings became Christian. Missionaries arrived in Viking territory from the 700s to the 800s. At first, many of them were Christian in name only and were content to mix pagan practices with Christianity. For some tribes, it took a few hundred years, but gradually many converted to true Christianity.

Can you think of other people in history who are known for defending the church? 1st century Christians martyred for their faith, C.S. Lewis, Charles Martel, Dietrich Bonhoeffer, Emperor Charlemagne, G.K. Chesterton, Godfrey of Bouillon, John Knox, King Alfred the Great.

Lesson 6

What does the word "defend" mean? Defend means to protect or keep someone from danger.

Lesson 7

Why do many people in Guibert's story have funny-sounding names? Because they are from a different time period and a different country. *Can you think of other medieval names?* Here are just a few: Adelaide, Estienne, Guiscard, Gwendolynn, Hildegard, Piers, Roland, Rowan, Yvain. (And then there are some more "normal" names like: Alice, Edmund, Eleanor, Frederick, John, Maria, Oliver, Roger, Rose, Walter, William.)

How did Guibert live the Third Commandment of Chivalry in this chapter? A few examples: he defended the boy being bullied, he was gentle to the boy by helping him, he defended Asceline.

Lesson 8

What are habits? They are regular/usual ways of behaving, routine behavior. *How is a habit important in learning the Third Commandment of Chivalry?* It's important to teach ourselves to do (and practice doing) the right thing over and over.

Lesson 9

What are some differences between Guibert's country and your country? Some differences in Guibert's country: it had different rules and laws, it was smaller, it didn't have grocery (or many other similar) stores…

How did Guibert show he cared about his native land in this story? Some examples: he didn't like those who threatened or attacked it, he loved the scenery, he was proud of the things made there and its important sites, he was proud of the good leader his land had.

Lesson 11

How do you think Guibert's use of bravery to help Asceline was more chivalrous than if he had just been defending himself? He was chivalrous by being selfless, in thinking about how to help Asceline and protecting her.

Lesson 12

Can bravery ever be wrong? Yes. *What might bad bravery look like?* A couple of examples are: being brave by trying to prove you're tough (perhaps even by hurting someone) or being brave for a bad cause.

Unscramble the words: BRAVE, WOLVES, STRONG, DEFEND.

Lesson 13

How did Guibert defend the weak (Third Commandment of Chivalry) and show courage (Fifth Commandment) in this chapter? #3: He helped defend Asceline and helped her to be safe first. #5: He fought the wolves.

How did Asceline defend the weak (Third Commandment) and show courage (Fifth Commandment) in this chapter? #3: She thought of a way to help the younger boy get to a safer place and helped defend against the wolves. #5: She fought the wolves.

What were crusaders? They were knights or soldiers going on a crusade to defend the Holy Land in an offensive or defensive war against Islamic forces.

Where were the crusaders Guibert met traveling to? The Holy Land: Jerusalem.

Lesson 14

Do you remember reading about the difference between the ideal type of Chivalry and the history type of Chivalry in Lesson 2? What are some ways the ideal of the Sixth Commandment of Chivalry is different from its history type of chivalry for this commandment? History type of chivalry for the sixth commandment was to go fight crusades or wars. The ideal, however, is to defend the holy God and fight Satan.

Lesson 15

Do you think castles had secret passages? Many did. *Why would a castle have a secret passage?* For a variety of reasons, including: so those inside could escape during an attack, so they could get supplies inside during a siege, so people or things could move in secret without being widely seen…

Answers to the crossword puzzle.

Lesson 16

Why is it so hard to be consistent and dependable in our duty? It is work, and work is hard too. Our sin nature does not want to do work. Also, Satan will sometimes work against our efforts to follow God.

Does God owe us anything? He doesn't. *How does your answer to that question make His consistent, dependable love for us so much more amazing?* We owe Him everything! This shows even more how incredible our God is.

How can being faithful, consistent, and dependable change the world for the better? We are following Christ's example. This usually makes life better for us, but more importantly, it changes the world for the better.

Lesson 17

How did telling the truth end up helping Guibert? Sir Enguerrand believed him later because he knew him to be truthful.

Answers to the quest of the day.

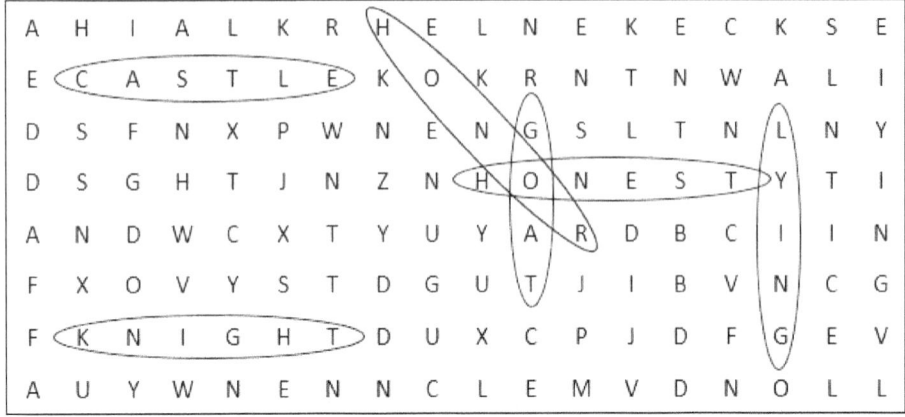

Lesson 18

Read John 8:44. "You are of your father the devil, and your will is to do your father's desires. He was a murderer from the beginning, and does not stand in the truth, because there is no truth in him. When he lies, he speaks out of his own character, for he is a liar and the father of lies." *What nickname does Jesus give the devil in this verse? Why do you think the devil is called that?* Jesus especially calls the devil a liar and "the father of lies." He was the first in the world to tell a lie and continues to lie even now. If we lie we are following the devil as a father rather than following God in telling the truth.

Quest of the day. Some examples of truthful, trustworthy, and honorable people: Abraham Lincoln, George Washington, William Wilberforce, Robert E. Lee, Mother Theresa, C.S. Lewis, Sergeant York, Theodore Roosevelt, Sam Houston.

Lesson 19

Guibert's thought-trail to the treasure:
   a) Dame Blanche complained often of strange noises in the castle walls.
   b) Sir Enguerrand said he was descended from Asgeir, the Viking who roved near Rouen.
   c) Nobody knew what happened to Asgeir's treasure.
   d) Sir Enguerrand inherited the castle from his grandsires, one of whom was Asgeir.
   e) Sir Talcott was plotting to marry Asceline for reasons unknown. Those reasons included getting access to Château Bon-heur. He would want the castle especially if he knew already there was treasure hidden there.
   f) Sir Talcott recruited his nephew Chrétien as a spy to search for the treasure he suspected was in Château Bon-heur.

g) Chrétien was tapping on the walls with a hammer, probably trying to find hollow places treasure could hide.

h) Ratramnus' trip from the drain into the secret passage of the wall showed that there were hollows behind the walls of the passage a man might hide things in.

Lesson 21

What does justice mean? Justice is bad acts getting punished and good acts being rewarded in the proper ways.

Lesson 22

How will you learn what's right and what's wrong? Some ways to learn right and wrong: from the Bible, your parents, your church/pastor, good books…

Why is knowing what's right and wrong important to helping bring justice to the world? We need to know this so we can know what the good to work for is and what the bad is to oppose. It does no good to work for something if it's not the right (Godly) thing.

Appendix B: The Ten Commandments of Chivalry

The Ten Commandments of Chivalry Updated
1. You shall believe and obey the Bible, and shall devote yourself to Christ.
2. You shall defend the church.
3. You shall be gentle to those weaker than you, and become their selfless defender wherever you find them.
4. You shall love your country.
5. You shall not recoil before the enemy.
6. You shall make ceaseless war against the enemies of Truth, and relentlessly work to take the gates of hell by storm.
7. You shall faithfully perform your responsibilities and shall honor all your commitments.
8. You shall be honest and keep your word.
9. You shall be generous, and give largesse to everyone.
10. You shall always be the champion of the right and the good, and oppose injustice and evil whenever and wherever you find it.

Léon Gautier's Original Ten Commandments of Chivalry
1. Thou shalt believe all that the Church teaches, and shalt observe all its directions.
2. Thou shalt defend the Church
3. Thou shalt respect all weaknesses, and shalt constitute thyself the defender of them.
4. Thou shalt love the country in which thou wast born.
5. Thou shalt not recoil before the enemy.
6. Thou shalt make war against the Infidel without cessation, and without mercy.
7. Thou shalt perform scrupulously thy feudal duties, if they be not contrary to the laws of God.
8. Thou shalt never lie, and shalt remain faithful to thy pledged word.
9. Thou shalt be generous, and give largesse to everyone.
10. Thou shalt be everywhere and always the champion of the Right and the Good against Injustice and Evil.

Further Reading

Books for Younger Students

Crafts/hands-on
Design Your Own Coat of Arms: An Introduction to Heraldry by Rosemary A. Chorzempa (Dover Children's Activity Books)
Make this Medieval Castle by Iain Ashman (Usborne cut-out models)
Make this Medieval Village by Iain Ashman (Usborne cut-out models)
The Usborne Castles Sticker Book by Abigail Wheatley and Rachel Firth

Fiction Picture books
A Medieval Feast by Aliki (Reading Rainbow Book)
Marguerite Makes a Book by Bruce Robertson
Reynard the Fox adapted and illustrated by Alain Vaes
Saint George and the Dragon by Margaret Hodges

Miscellaneous
The Book of Virtues: A Treasury of Great Moral Stories by William J. Bennet
The Stars: A New Way to See Them by H.A. Rey

Non-fiction picture books
A Day with a Troubadour by Régine Pernoud
A Street Through Time by Steve Noon
A Tournament of Knights by Joe Lasker
Castles by Philip Steele (Kingfisher Books)
Cross Sections: Castle by Stephen Biesty
Fly Guy Presents Castles by Ted Arnold
In the Time of Knights by Shelley Tanaka
Knights and Castles Illuminated by Philip Dixon
Living History Knights in Armor by John D Care, ed.
The Making of a Knight by Patrick O'Brien
The Medieval Castle by A.G. Smith (Dover History Coloring Book)
The Usborne Time Traveler's Knights and Castles by Judy Hindley

Pop-up Books
Squire Dan's First Joust by Dereen Taylor

Knights: A 3-Dimensional Exploration by John Howe

Knight: a Noble Guide for Young Squires by Sir Geoffrey de Lance

Books for Older Students

Chivalry
Chivalry by Leon Gautier

Maxims of Christian Chivalry by Kenelm Digby, edited by Nicholas Dillon

Fiction
Men of Iron by Howard Pyle

Son of Charlemagne by Barbara Willard

The Black Arrow by Robert Louis Stevenson

The Boy's King Arthur by Sidney Lanier, illustrated by N.C. Wyeth

The Story of King Arthur and His Knights by Howard Pyle

The White Company by Arthur Conan Doyle, illustrated by N.C. Wyeth

Yvain: Knight of the Lion by M.T. Anderson and Andrea Offermann (Graphic Novel)

History
Daily Life in Medieval Times by Joseph and Frances Gies

Herbs for the Mediaeval Household for Cooking Healing and Divers Uses by Margaret B. Freeman

Medieval Swordsmanship: Illustrated Methods and Techniques by John Clements

Medieval Wordbook by Madeleine Pelner Cosman

Revelations: the Medieval World by James Harpur and Elizabeth Hallman

Source Book of Mediæval History by Frederic A. Ogg

The History of the Kings of England by Geoffrey of Monmouth

The New Concise History of the Crusades by Thomas Madden

The Normans: Warrior Knights and their Castles by Christopher Gravett and David Nicholle (Osprey)

Two Lives of Charlemagne by Einhard and Notker the Stammerer

Endnotes-Works Cited

Parent's Note

[i] Smith, Morton H. *Harmony of the Westminster Confession and Catechisms.* Presbyterian Press. 2010. p. 11

[ii] Duby, George. *William Marshal the Flower of Chivalry.* Translated by Richard Howard. New York, NY: Pantheon Books. 1985. p. 55

Lesson 1

[iii] Pyle, Howard. *Men of Iron.* Bob Jones University Press. Greenville, South Carolina. 1993. p. 8

[iv] Pyle, Howard. *Men of Iron.* Bob Jones University Press. Greenville, South Carolina. 1993. p. 27

[v] Forgette, Steven. "Quotes about Chivalry & Knighthood." The International Fellowship of Chivalry-Now. Web. 7 February 2019. www.chivalrynow.net/articles/steven.htm

[vi] McKay, Brett and Kate McKay. *The Art of Manliness—Manvotionals: Timeless Wisdom and Advice on Living the 7 Manly Virtues.* How Books. Cincinnati, OH. 2011. p. 23

Lesson 2

[vii] "Bil Keane Quotes." BrainyQuote.com. BrainyMedia Inc, 2019. 18 February 2019. https://www.brainyquote.com/quotes/bil_keane_121860

[viii] "Chivalry Sayings and Quotes." Wise Old Sayings. Web. 18 February 2019. www.wiseoldsayings.com/chivalry-quotes

[ix] "Saint George and the Dragon Quotes." Goodreads.com. Margaret Hodges. 1 April 2019. www.goodreads.com/work/quotes/2042811-saint-george-and-the-dragon

[x] "Picture Quotes." Picturequotes.com. Edmund Spenser. 1 April 2019. www.picturequotes.com/saint-george-shalt-called-bee-saint-george-of-mery-england-the-sign-of-victoree-quote-73376

[xi] "20 Awesome Quotes About Salvation." Christianquotes.info. A.W. Tozer. 1 April 2019. www.christianquotes.info/top-quotes/20-awesome-quotes-salvation

Lesson 4

[xii] Digby, Kenhelm. *Maxims of Christian Chivalry.* Catholic Authors Press. Hartford:Ct. 2003. p. 11

Lesson 5

[xiii] "Ovid Quotes." BrainyQuote.com. BrainyMedia Inc, 2019. 9 February 2019. https://www.brainyquote.com/quotes/ovid_159362

[xiv] "John Calvin Quotes." BrainyQuote.com. BrainyMedia Inc, 2019. 9 February 2019. https://www.brainyquote.com/quotes/john_calvin_144215

Lesson 6

[xv] "Top 10 Quotes on the Church by Martin Luther King Jr." Juicyecumenism.com. 9 February 2019. www.juicyecumenism.com/2016/01/18/top-10-quotes-church-martin-luther-king-jr

xvi "Charles Spurgeon on Defending the Faith." Apologeticsindex.org. David Kowalski. 9 February 2019. www.apologeticsindex.org/3030-spurgeon-defending-the-faith

xvii "Apologetics Quotes." Always Be Ready Apologetics Ministry. 9 February 2019. www.alwaysbeready.com/quotations

Lesson 7

xviii Gies, Frances. *The Knight in History.* Harper & Row Publishers, New York, NY. 1984. p. 79

xix "Quotable Quote." Goodreads.com. Web. 9 February 2019. www.goodreads.com/quotes/381406-defend-the-weak-protect-both-young-and-old-never-desert

xx Shakespeare, William. *Measure for Measure.* Online Library of Liberty. 9 February 2019. www.oll.libertyfund.org/quote/109

xxi "Anne Bronte Quotes." BrainyQuote.com. BrainyMedia Inc, 2019. 9 February 2019. https://www.brainyquote.com/quotes/anne_bronte_553961

xxii "Chivalry Sayings and Quotes." Wise Old Sayings. Web. 18 February 2019. www.wiseoldsayings.com/chivalry-quotes

Lesson 8

xxiii "Charles Kingsley Quotes." BrainyQuote.com. BrainyMedia Inc, 2019. 12 February 2019. https://www.brainyquote.com/quotes/charles_kingsley_403825

xxiv Bennet, William J. *The Book of Virtues: A Treasury of Great Moral Stories.* Simon and Schuster: New York, NY. 1993. p. 217

xxv "Strength Quotes." Notable Quotes. Web. 18 February 2019. www.notable-quotes.com/s/strength_quotes

xxvi "Strength Quotes." Notable Quotes. Web. 18 February 2019. www.notable-quotes.com/s/strength_quotes

xxvii Watson, Thomas. *All Things for Good.* The Banner of Truth Trust. 2011.

Lesson 9

xxix "4th of July Quotes for Students and Children." 4to40. Web. 1 April 1, 2019. www.4to40.com/quotations/famous-english-quotes/4th-of-july-quotes-in-english

xxix "Winston S. Churchill Quotes." Goodreads.com. Web. 15 February 2019. https://www.goodreads.com/quotes/97957-we-shall-go-on-to-the-end-we-shall-fight

xxx "Patriotism Quotes." Notable Quotes. Web. 18 February 2019. www.notable-quotes.com/p/patriotism_quotes

xxxi Thorpe, Lewis, translator. *The History of the Kings of Britain* by Geoffrey of Monmouth. Penguin Classics: London, England. 1966. p. 216

Lesson 10

xxxii "Ronald Reagan Quotes." BrainyQuote.com. BrainyMedia Inc, 2019. 10 February 2019. https://www.brainyquote.com/quotes/ronald_reagan_147696

xxxiii "Patriotism Quotes." Notable Quotes. Web. 18 February 2019. www.notable-quotes.com/p/patriotism_quotes

xxxiv Bennet, William J. *The Book of Virtues: A Treasury of Great Moral Stories.* Simon and Schuster: New York, NY. 1993. p. 713

Endnotes: Works Cited

Lesson 11

xxxv "John Wayne Quotes." BrainyQuote.com. BrainyMedia Inc, 2019. 10 February 2019. https://www.brainyquote.com/quotes/john_wayne_161631

xxxvi "The Wizard of Oz." IMDb. Web. 18 February 2019. https://www.imdb.com/title/tt0032138/characters/nm0481618

xxxvii Duby, George. Richard Howard translator. *William Marshal the Flower of Chivalry*. New York, NY: Pantheon Books. 1985. p. 69

xxxviii "Lao Tzu Quotes." BrainyQuote.com. BrainyMedia Inc, 2019. 10 February 2019. https://www.brainyquote.com/quotes/lao_tzu_101043

xxxix Lewis, C.S. *The Horse and His Boy*. HarperCollins Publishers: NY. 2000

Lesson 12

xl "George S. Patton Quotes." BrainyQuote.com. BrainyMedia Inc, 2019. 25 February 2019. https://www.brainyquote.com/quotes/george_s_patton_104742

xli "Billy Graham Quotes." BrainyQuote.com. BrainyMedia Inc, 2019. 25 February 2019. https://www.brainyquote.com/quotes/billy_graham_113622

xlii "Helen Keller Quotes." BrainyQuote.com. BrainyMedia Inc, 2019. 12 February 2019. https://www.brainyquote.com/quotes/helen_keller_162480

xliii McKay, Brett and Kate McKay. *The Art of Manliness—Manvotionals: Timeless Wisdom and Advice on Living the 7 Manly Virtues*. How Books. Cincinnati, OH. 2011. p. 17

Lesson 13

xliv Riley-Smith, Jonathan. "Crusading as an Act of Love." Published in *Medieval Religion by* Constance H. Berman. Psychology Press. 2005. p. 51

xlv Riley-Smith, Jonathan. "Crusading as an Act of Love." Published in *Medieval Religion* by Constance H. Berman. Psychology Press. 2005. p. 54

xlvi "G.K. Chesterton Quotable Quotes." Goodreads.com. Web. 11 February 2019. www.goodreads.com/quotes/94304-the-true-soldier-fights-not-because-he-hates-what-is

Lesson 14

xlvii "Apologetics Quotes." Always Be Ready Apologetics Ministry. Web. 9 February 2019. www.alwaysbeready.com/quotations

xlviii "Apologetics Quotes." Always Be Ready Apologetics Ministry. Web. 9 February 2019. www.alwaysbeready.com/quotations

xlix "Elvis Presley Quotes." BrainyQuote.com. BrainyMedia Inc, 2019. 18 February 2019. https://www.brainyquote.com/quotes/elvis_presley_133068

l "Winston Churchill Quotes." BrainyQuote.com. BrainyMedia Inc, 2019. 18 February 2019. https://www.brainyquote.com/quotes/winston_churchill_129864

li "George S. Patton Quotes." BrainyQuote.com. BrainyMedia Inc, 2019. 18 February 2019. https://www.brainyquote.com/quotes/george_s_patton_143700

Lesson 15

lii Forgette, Steven. "Quotes about Chivalry & Knighthood." The International Fellowship of Chivalry-Now. Web. 7 February 2019. www.chivalrynow.net/articles/steven.htm

liii "Dependability Sayings and Quotes." Wise Old Sayings online. Web. 11 February 2019. www.wiseoldsayings.com/dependability-quotes/

liv "George Washington Quotes." BrainyQuote.com. BrainyMedia Inc, 2019. 12 February 2019. https://www.brainyquote.com/quotes/george_washington_161339

lv "4th of July Quotes for Students and Children." 4to40. Web. 1 April 1, 2019. www.4to40.com/quotations/famous-english-quotes/4th-of-july-quotes-in-english

lvi McKay, Brett and Kate McKay. *The Art of Manliness—Manvotionals: Timeless Wisdom and Advice on Living the 7 Manly Virtues.* How Books. Cincinnati, OH. 2011. p. 22

lvii McKay, Brett and Kate McKay. *The Art of Manliness—Manvotionals: Timeless Wisdom and Advice on Living the 7 Manly Virtues.* How Books. Cincinnati, OH. 2011. p. 15

lviii "John D. Rockefeller Quotes." BrainyQuote.com. BrainyMedia Inc, 2019. 12 February 2019. https://www.brainyquote.com/quotes/john_d_rockefeller_107564

Lesson 17

lix "Thomas Jefferson Quotes." BrainyQuote.com. BrainyMedia Inc, 2019. 12 February 2019. https://www.brainyquote.com/quotes/thomas_jefferson_101007.

lx "James E. Faust Quotes." BrainyQuote.com. BrainyMedia Inc, 2019. 12 February 2019. https://www.brainyquote.com/quotes/james_e_faust_621206

lxi "Pierre Corneille Quotes." BrainyQuote.com. BrainyMedia Inc, 2019. 12 February 2019. https://www.brainyquote.com/quotes/pierre_corneille_117892

lxii McKay, Brett and Kate McKay. *The Art of Manliness—Manvotionals: Timeless Wisdom and Advice on Living the 7 Manly Virtues.* How Books. Cincinnati, OH. 2011. P. 9

Lesson 18

lxiii "Charles Dickens Quotes." BrainyQuote.com. BrainyMedia Inc, 2019. 18 February 2019. https://www.brainyquote.com/quotes/charles_dickens_154086

lxiv "96 Honesty Quotes." Inspirational Words of Wisdom. Web. 18 February 2019. https://www.wow4u.com/honesty-quotes/

lxv "96 Honesty Quotes." Inspirational Words of Wisdom. Web. 18 February 2019. https://www.wow4u.com/honesty-quotes/

lxvi "96 Honesty Quotes." Inspirational Words of Wisdom. Web. 18 February 2019. https://www.wow4u.com/honesty-quotes/

Lesson 19

lxvii Price, Brian R. *Ramon Lull's Book of Knighthood & Chivalry & the anonymous Ordene de Chevalerie.* The Chivalry Bookshelf. 2001. Translated from William Caxton's 1484 translation of the text in Middle English.

Endnotes: Works Cited

[lxviii] Thorpe, Lewis, translator. *The History of the Kings of Britain* by Geoffrey of Monmouth. Penguin Classics: London, England. 1966. p. 212

[lxix] Swan, Charles and Wynnard Hooper, Translators and Editors. *Gesta Romanorum: or Entertaining Moral Stories*. Dover Publications: Toronto, Ontario. 1959. p. 332

[lxx] Ogg, Frederic Austin. *Sourcebook of Medieval History*. London, England: 1907. p. 114

Lesson 20

[lxxi] Dela Cruz, Stephen. "10 of the Most Powerful Generosity Quotes and Why You Need Them." Medium.com. Web. 2017. https://bit.ly/2CN37XR. 16 October 2018

[lxxii] Dela Cruz, Stephen. "10 of the Most Powerful Generosity Quotes and Why You Need Them." Medium.com. Web. 2017. https://bit.ly/2CN37XR. 16 October 2018

[lxxiii] Dela Cruz, Stephen. "10 of the Most Powerful Generosity Quotes and Why You Need Them." Medium.com. Web. 2017. https://bit.ly/2CN37XR. 16 October 2018

[lxxiv] Dela Cruz, Stephen. "10 of the Most Powerful Generosity Quotes and Why You Need Them." Medium.com. Web. 2017. https://bit.ly/2CN37XR. 16 October 2018

[lxxv] "Bleak House Quotes." Goodreads.com. Web. 14 April 2019. www.goodreads.com/work/quotes/2960365

Lesson 21

[lxxvi] Price, Brian R. *Ramon Lull's Book of Knighthood & Chivalry & the anonymous Ordene de Chevalerie*. The Chivalry Bookshelf. 2001. Translated from William Caxton's 1484 translation of the text in Middle English. p. 77

[lxxvii] Digby, Kenhelm. *Maxims of Christian Chivalry*. Catholic Authors Press. Hartford:Ct. 2003. p. 5

Lesson 22

[lxxviii] Pyle, Howard. *The Story of Sir Launcelot and his Companions*. Wildside Press, 1907.

[lxxviii] Pyle, Howard. *The Story of Sir Launcelot and his Companions*. Wildside Press, 1907.

Further Quote Sources

All Léon Gautier quotes are from *Chivalry: The Everyday Life of the Medieval Knight*. Crescent Books: New York, NY. 1989.